WITHDRAWN

ECOLOGY AND EVOLUTION OF
AN ANDEAN HUMMINGBIRD
(Oreotrochilus estella)

ECOLOGY AND EVOLUTION OF AN ANDEAN HUMMINGBIRD
(Oreotrochilus estella)

BY

F. LYNN CARPENTER

UNIVERSITY OF CALIFORNIA PRESS
BERKELEY • LOS ANGELES • LONDON
1976

University of California Publications in Zoology

Volume 106
Approved for publication April 4, 1975
Issued September 17, 1976

University of California Press
Berkeley and Los Angeles
California

University of California Press, Ltd.
London, England

591.08
C153u
v. 106
1976

ISBN: 0-520-09545-6
Library of Congress Catalog Card Number: 75-620056

© 1976 by The Regents of the University of California
Printed in the United States of America

Contents

Abstract	1
Acknowledgments	2
Introduction	2
I. Statement of the problem	2
II. The study subject and its environment	5
Characteristics of Study Area and Study Periods	7
Methods of Behavioral Studies on *O. estella*	9
Morphological Adaptations	10
I. Size and color	10
II. Discussion: adaptive values of size and color	13
Behavioral Adaptations: Foraging and Roosting	16
I. Ground- and rock-dwelling habits	16
II. Discussion: adaptiveness and comparative aspects of foraging and roosting behavior	22
Reproductive Adaptations	25
I. Reproduction	25
II. Discussion: seasonal reproduction, nest sites, and winter mortality	30
Territorial Adaptations	34
I. Breeding season territories	34
II. The male during the breeding season	36
III. Winter feeding areas and territories	37
IV. Discussion: comparative aspects of territoriality	38
Energetics	43
I. Metabolism and torpor	43
II. Energetics model for feeding territoriality	50
III. Energetics of locomotion	51
IV. Energy budget of *O. estella*	53
V. Interspecific interactions	60
Concluding Discussion	61
I. *O. estella* in the high Andes — a synthesis	61
II. The taxon cycle in *Oreotrochilus*	63
III. Evolution and colonization at high altitudes	65
IV. Conclusion	67
Literature Cited	68
Plates	75

List of Tables

Table	1.	Climate at 4000 m in southern Peru and northern Chile. 8
	2.	Distribution of intensive observation hours in the field 9
	3.	Tarsus and toenail measurements 12
	4.	Change of perch site with change in temperature. 22
	5.	Nesting success in hummingbirds 32
	6.	Comparison of body size, regulated body temperature and minimum ambient temperatures for five species of hummingbirds 49
	7.	Calculated cost of linear flight for four hummingbirds 52
	8.	Time allotments for activities on a 24 hour basis. 54
	9A.	Energy allotments for activities on a 24 hour basis 55
	B.	Assumptions and methods of calculation in Table 9A. 56
	10.	Comparison of energy expenditures of *O. estella* and a hypothetical hummingbird, both in *Chuquiraga* in the winter 58
	11.	Relative values of three adaptive traits of *O. estella* 59

List of Figures

Figure	1.	Map of the distribution of *Oreotrochilus* taxa 4
	2.	Map of the study areas 6
	3.	Size distribution of 166 species of hummingbirds 11
	4.	Distribution of wing disc loading in 74 species of hummingbirds 11
	5.	Seasonal changes in frequency of types of feeding behavior 17
	6.	Pollination of *Chuquiraga spinosa* 18
	7.	The insect food of *O. estella* .19
	8.	Thermal microclimate in nest and roost sites 21
	9.	Breeding season 26
	10.	Population sizes of *O. estella* .27
	11.	Model of selection pressures affecting the territorial systems of *O. estella* 39
	12.	Metabolism in *Oreotrochilus estella* 45
	13.	Relation of T_b to T_a in homeothermy and in torpor 46
	14.	Oxygen consumption in torpor 47

ECOLOGY AND EVOLUTION OF AN ANDEAN HUMMINGBIRD

By

F. Lynn Carpenter

Abstract

Oreotrochilus estella is one of the few hummingbird species living above 4000 m in the Peruvian Andes where vegetation is sparse and the climate rigorous. This species has evolved characteristics very different from those of other hummingbirds whose habitat is generally tropical lowlands and whose habits are usually arboreal. I studied *O. estella* in the field in southern Peru and northern Chile and in the laboratory at the University of California, Berkeley, to determine the magnitude of these differences.

O. estella weighs 8 gm, unusually large for a hummingbird. Large size reduces short-term stresses on homeotherms in cold climates by reducing the surface–volume ratio. The feet of *O. estella* are much larger than those of other similarly sized hummingbirds. Barren high altitudes have imposed terrestrial habits on this species and stronger feet are thus required. *O. estella* is atypical in its preference to perch while flower-feeding and while gleaning small invertebrates from the ground. Perching saves energy, especially at very high altitudes where thin air causes a larger energy demand for hovering flight.

O. estella roosts by clinging to vertical or overhanging surfaces among rocks. Winter roosts are more protected from cold and wind than are summer roosts. Field and laboratory studies showed that lowering of the ambient temperature causes the birds to seek more sheltered roosts.

Females build nests during the rainy summer in sheltered areas among rocky gorges in sites similar to the roost sites. Protection from severe weather and possibly from nest predators has selected for great specificity in nest sites. Nesting success rate was two to four times higher in *O. estella* than in seven species of hummingbirds in California and Central America. Competition for suitable nest sites was aggressive and intense, implying that the population size is regulated partly by nest-site availability.

In the breeding season (summer) females defended nesting and feeding territories, but the males seemed aterritorial. This is the reverse of the territorial system in other sexually dimorphic hummingbirds. Apparently *O. estella* is atypical because the nest-site requirements of the females force them to occupy the gorges, which also possess the richest food supplies; because the female is territorial she forces the male onto the open hillsides where food is so widely dispersed that territorial defense is impossible. The males occasionally visited females in the gorges, attempting to display and mate with them. This is the reverse of other hummingbirds, in which courting usually occurs on the male's territory. Adult males seemed to have a home range that included a gorge of one or more nesting females – this is similar to the system in another high-montane species in Central America.

Both males and females aggressively defended feeding territories in the winter non-breeding season if the food supply was rich in energy (*Eucalyptus*), but not if it was poor, as was the case with the only native "bird-flower" that bloomed in the study areas during the winter, *Chuquiraga spinosa* (Compositae), probably because the low attractiveness of *Chuquiraga* resulted in few challenges.

Vocalizations seemed to play the most important role in territorial defense. Thus, the male's large size and bright colors probably have been selected for a striking courtship display, rather than for aggressive territorial displays as in other hummingbirds. However, it is suggested that the more important selection pressure for large size in the male was the dispersion of his food sources in the summer: the necessity for long foraging flights selects for relatively larger size in males because large size results in more efficient linear flight.

Resting and torpid metabolism in *O. estella* were measured as a basis for calculating energy budgets from time budgets. The cost of both linear and hovering flight was estimated from theoretical and empirical equations. An energetics model of feeding territoriality was derived. Time and energy budgets were then computed for both sexes at different times of the year. Most energy was spent by breeding females, cost increasing as the young matured. Individuals using *Chuquiraga* in the winter spent least energy because they did not defend territories or flycatch, they invariably perched to feed, and they spent at least nine hours fully torpid each night. *O. estella* spends 1.3 to 4 times more energy than does *Calypte anna* because *O. estella* is twice as large, its food supply is more dispersed spatially, and it occupies regions of generally lower ambient temperature. When an energy budget was calculated for a hypothetical "typical" hummingbird in *O. estella*'s high-altitude environment, its energy budget was nearly 3 times higher than that of *O. estella*. A comparison of the budget of *O. estella* with the hypothetical budget revealed those adaptations of *O. estella* which conserve the most energy.

Acknowledgments

This study was completed as partial fulfillment of the requirements for Doctor of Philosophy at the University of California at Berkeley. Special thanks go to Dr. Oliver P. Pearson, who gave guidance through my doctoral research and contributed the germs for many of the ideas in this paper. The ideas and efforts of many other people also contributed, among them D. F. Bradford, R. K. Colwell, J. H. Hunt, C. Koford, E. Koford, R. E. MacMillen, P. Bunnell, and C. H. F. Rowell. Gracious hospitality in Peru was offered by Dr. Hernando de Macedo, Sr. Humfredo de Macedo, Sra. Emma de Paredes, Sr. M. Plenge, and Sr. L. Ramirez. Dr. R. Ferreyra aided in plant identification. D. Helmgren and E. Cova gave technical assistance. E. Reid and D. Littler prepared the more complex figures. The referees chosen by the Editor were especially thorough and helpful. Financial assistance came from the Museum of Vertebrate Zoology, University of California at Berkeley, and from a grant from the Chapman Memorial Fund of the American Museum of Natural History, New York.

Introduction
I. STATEMENT OF THE PROBLEM

Studies of evolution and adaptations often deal with populations of organisms that have been isolated geographically from an ancestral unit. Indeed, Wallace and Darwin conceived their theory of evolution partly as a result of their observations on oceanic islands. The concept of geographic isolation extends to islands on land, such as mountain tops (Brown, 1971). To study the evolution and adaptations of a given species, whether or not it is geographically isolated now, one needs to know: (1) what the characteristics of the ancestral taxon were, (2) what environmental pressures the ancestors experienced, and (3) what environmental pressures the species in question experiences. Ideally, for such a study, the species should occupy a habitat that is very different in its biological and physical characteristics from that of its probable ancestors, thereby promoting evolution away from the ancestral type.

An excellent study case is presented by the hummingbird family, Trochilidae. Pitelka (1942) commented on the uniformity of "general life habits among hummingbirds — a uniformity perhaps as extreme as that in any other taxonomic group of similar rank." A majority of the more than 300 species are lowland or low montane, tropical or subtropical birds existing in heavily vegetated habitats where seasonal and diurnal temperature fluctuations are small. Even most temperate zone hummingbirds are migratory and become tropical for half the year. Arboreality, lack of perching ability, foraging by hovering, maneuverability, and nesting habits are all suited for agile life and successful reproduction in dense vegetation. The predominant plumage color is iridescent yellowish green, especially dorsally, which although jewel-like when a specimen is hand-held, can be quite cryptic in the green habitat. Hummingbirds lay a clutch of two eggs. The consistent, small clutch size is typical of tropical birds; the selection pressures causing this are unknown although there are several hypotheses (for review see Krebs, 1972; also Cody, 1966; Ricklefs, 1970). Most tropical birds show variation in clutch size across habitats, but hummingbirds do not. These then are the general adaptive characteristics of the family.

Less than 30 species of hummingbirds have geographic ranges beyond 35° latitude (Greenewalt, 1960a: xv; Grant and Grant, 1968). Even fewer occur in boreal life zones. There is only one genus known to reside permanently, entirely, and abundantly above treeline, and that is the South American genus *Oreotrochilus* of the high Andes. The four (± 1) species of the genus are distributed along the Andean mountain chain from central Chile to northern Ecuador, their altitudinal range increasing with increasing proximity to the equator [1550-3700 m in Chile up to 3700-5000 m in Ecuador (Ruschi, 1961a; Johson, 1967; Rhoads, 1912, cited in Vuilleumier, 1966; Museum of Vertebrate Zoology specimens)]. Generally, the members of the genus encounter the following environmental characteristics:

1. Vegetation comprised of grasses, or occasionally, low scrubby growth (páramo in north, puna in south)
2. Climate characterized by extremes of temperature and humidity
3. Rugged mountainous topography and isolated habitats
4. Low oxygen availability and air of low density

These environmental characteristics differ from those encountered by the vast majority of hummingbird species. These characteristics combine to form a potentially stressful environment for small, homeothermic nectarivores and insectivores such as hummingbirds because of high energy costs coupled with food resources that are scarce or that fluctuate in time and space.

Since the Andes are a relatively new geological formation, the major uplifts having occurred two to ten million years ago (Hollingworth and Rutland, 1968), and because the South American continental shield is very old, it is safe to assume that habitat suitable for bird life has been available for a long time in the lowlands but became available only recently in the Andes. Thus, the ancestor to the genus *Oreotrochilus* probably came from the lowland tropics east of the great mountain chain and shared the characteristics described above for the generalized, or "typical," hummingbird. One would expect that in

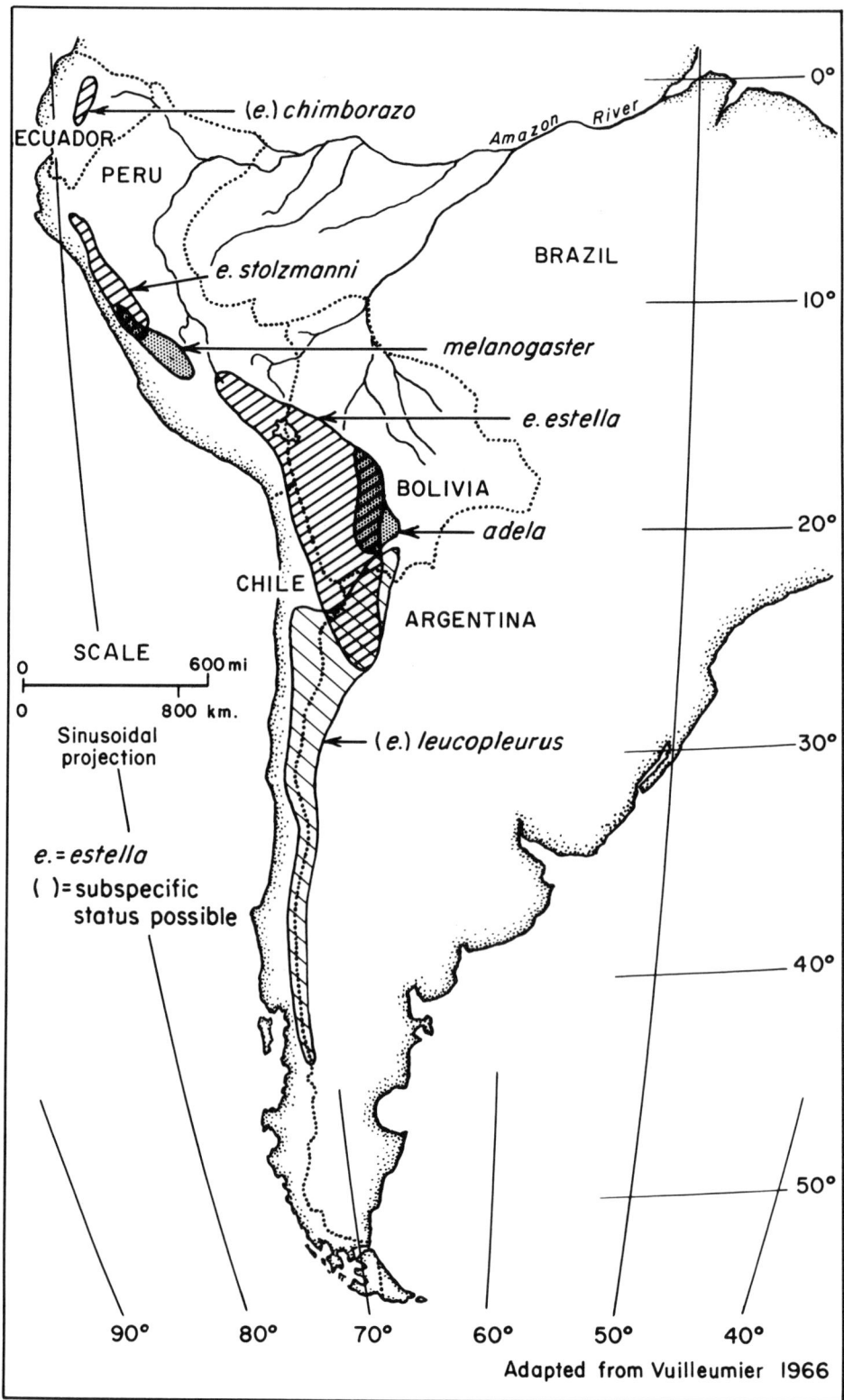

Fig. 1. Distribution of *Oreotrochilus* taxa along the Andes of South America. Stippled areas are the isolated distributions of the two melanistic species; hatch marks indicate the various white-bellied forms.

facing the very different environmental characteristics offered by the Andes, this ancestral type evolved special morphological, physiological, and behavioral adaptations. The *Oreotrochilus* of today, then, should show striking differences from the typical hummingbirds of the lowlands from which it was, and still is, isolated geographically. The subject of this study is the direction and magnitude of these changes in a member of a family noted for its relative homogeneity.

II. THE STUDY SUBJECT AND ITS ENVIRONMENT

The species of *Oreotrochilus* may be divided into two groups (Fig. 1). One is composed of two melanistic species with restricted ranges: *O. adela* in Bolivia and *O. melanogaster* in central Peru. The second group is quite complex and consists of one (Zimmer, 1951), two (de Schauensee, 1966; 1970), or three (Vuilleumier, 1966) species that are somewhat clinally variable along the length of the Andes: (1) *O. leucopleurus* (or *O. estella leucopleurus*) ranges from central Chile and adjacent Argentina to northern Chile and northwest Argentina; (2) *O. estella* (including subspecies *estella* and *stolzmanni*) ranges from northwest Argentina through Bolivia and northernmost Chile to northern Peru; and (3) *O. chimborazo* (or *O. estella chimborazo*) occurs on isolated mountaintops throughout Ecuador. All of these forms have white bellies and white in the tail, and all except *O. chimborazo* have essentially identical iridescent throat markings. Since none of these three forms has been shown convincingly to overlap with any other of the three, and since they are similar to one another in many ways, Zimmer (1951) considers them all to be subspecies of *O. estella*. In any event, the basic type of *O. estella* is apparently actively and probably quite recently differentiating along the entire axis of the Andes occupied by the genus. This is in contrast to the situation with *O. melanogaster* and *O. adela*, which are probably older forms (Vuilleumier, 1966), originally may have had connecting ranges, and are now restricted in range and apparently in numbers.

O. estella estella seemed the best choice among all *Oreotrochilus* forms for a study of evolution and adaptation because: (1) it is extremely abundant and easily found in its habitat; (2) its range is logistically accessible for study; (3) some pioneering work had already been done on its basic biology (Pearson, 1953; Dorst, 1956; 1962); and (4) it lives in habitat that is among the most physically rigorous of those occupied by any species in the genus (dry puna as opposed to wet, more moderate páramo).

Bowman (1916), Weberbauer (1945), and Vuilleumier (1966) have analyzed and reviewed works on the topography, climate, and vegetation of the Andes, including that of the puna of southern Peru and northern Chile where I concentrated my work. Here I will summarize their analyses and, immediately following the Introduction, present a section with details especially pertinent to the biology of *O. e. estella*.

In Peru the Andes form an undulating, broken chain running northwest to southeast. An east-west range, the Cordillera de Vilcanota, occurs at about 14°S latitude (Fig. 2). South of this range, the Andes separate into two parallel chains, the Cordillera Occidental (western range) and the Cordillera Oriental (eastern range). Between these great chains is a grassy, high-altitude plateau (the altiplano), averaging more than 4000 m above sea level. Its lowest parts are occupied by Lake Titicaca (3810 m) in Peru and Lake Poopoo (3688 m) in Bolivia. The vegetation of the altiplano and of its borders is composed mainly of several genera of bunchgrasses and is called "puna." Low-growing spiny or resinous plant species abound. The paucity of tall shrubs and trees may be explained in part by

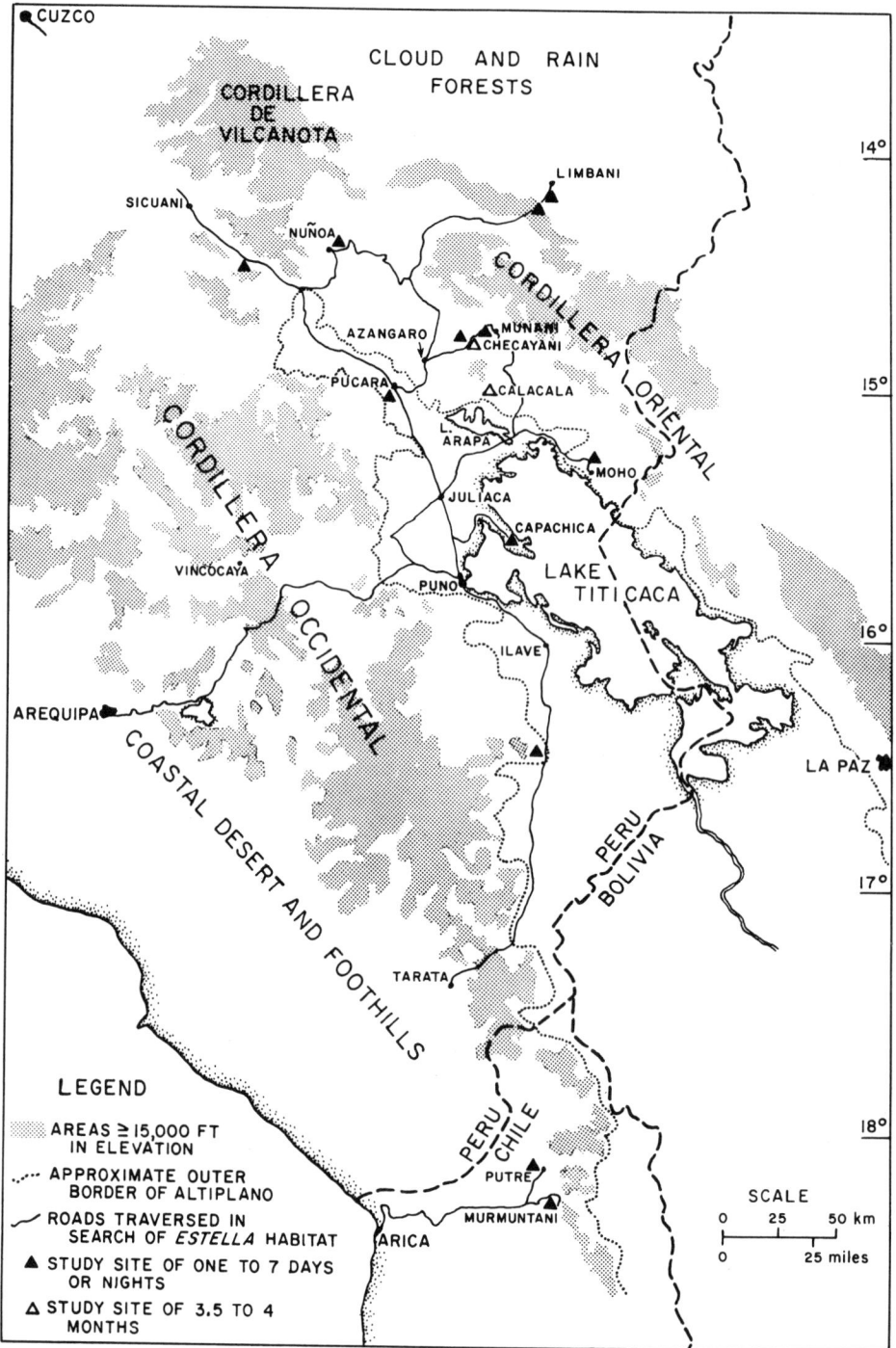

Fig. 2 Map showing the 3 major and 12 minor sites of this study from 1968 to 1971 in Peru and Chile. The vertical axis of the figure is north-south. Map is modified from USAF Operational Navigation Charts N-25 and P-26. The projection is conformal conic.

the climate of the altiplano. Precipitation is distinctly seasonal (Table 1). Total annual rainfall on the altiplano has been measured at Puno, Peru, to be about 1000 mm, the majority of which falls during five months of the year (Knoch, 1930, cited in Weberbauer, 1945). Four to six months are predictably and almost entirely dry (May through October). Diurnal range in temperature is great. In general throughout the southern Peruvian Andes, the warmest month is November and the coldest July. The line of permanent snow occurs between 5200 and 5800 m, but frosts occur regularly throughout the altiplano even during the wetter months and may occur as low as 2700 m on the western flank of the Cordillera Occidental. Hailstorms are common to the altiplano in the summer.

In studying the adaptations of *Oreotrochilus estella estella,* I concentrated on the morphology, behavior, and physiology of several populations of the species, both in the field and in the laboratory. Morphology and behavior are discussed in the first four sections of this work. These topics form the background for the synthetic fifth section on the energetics of the bird, since morphology, physiology, and behavior in conjunction with the biological and physical aspects of the environment determine both energy available to and energy expended by an organism. If an organism is to be successful, as *O. estella* is, its energetic resources and intake must balance the energetic costs of living and reproducing. How *O. estella* accomplishes this in comparison with the lowland members of its family is the major theme of this investigation.

Characteristics of Study Area and Study Periods

The largest numbers of *O. e. estella* are found on the 4000 m high altiplano and in its hilly borders, which reach to 4600 m or more, although *O. e. estella* is also found on the western flanks of the Cordillera Occidental down to 3000 m (Pearson, 1953, and pers. comm.) and on the eastern flanks of the Cordillera Oriental down to about 3700 m (Fig. 2). I concentrated my studies in the hilly borders of the altiplano between 14 and 16°S latitude, although I made some observations in northern Chile at 18°S. All study areas were between 3800 and 4600 m above sea level. *O. estella* is particularly concentrated in gorges and canyons cut into the hills by rapidly flowing streams. The sides of these gorges vary from gently sloping to quite steep, and are undercut by the stream or original river to form overhanging rock ledges and occasional cave openings (Plates 3, 4, 5). The gorges are separated from each other by rolling, open, grassy hillsides (puna) that are usually devoid of shrubs and trees but often have cacti nestled between the clumps of bunchgrass. The most characteristic genera of puna bunchgrasses are *Calamogrostis, Stipa,* and *Festuca* (Weberbauer, 1945).

Several other groups of flowering plants occur in the gorges, among rocks, or where there is some other shelter: ground-hugging Cactaceae (*Opuntia, Echinocactus, Echinopsis*), composite shrubs (*Baccharis, Lepidophyllum, Senecio, Chuquiraga* – see Plate 2), and perennial herbs such as *Lupinus* (Leguminosae), *Bomarea* (Amaryllidaceae; Plate 1), *Cajophora* (Loasaceae; Plate 1), *Siphocampylus* (Campanulaceae). Stands of the large treelike shrub, *Polylepis* spp. (Rosaceae, Plates 4, 5, 6), are widely dispersed and variable in habitat, sometimes occurring in the sheltered gorges, sometimes on open hillsides. Individuals may grow to 5 m tall, but form tangled thickets rather than true woodlands or forests. A tree, *Buddleia coriacea* (Loganiaceae), grows around human habitations. In addition, *Eucalyptus globulus* (Myrtaceae – Plate 7) has been introduced for its wood and grows in cultivation around human settlements at altitudes as high as 4025 m. Human activity has undoubtedly altered the vegetation of the altiplano during many centuries of

TABLE 1

Climate at 4000 m in Southern Peru and Northern Chile (14-18°S latitude)*
(Boxed months indicate extreme limits of the breeding season of *O. estella estella*)

Sept	Oct	Nov	Dec	Jan	Feb	Mar	Apr	May	June	July	Aug
"SPRING"			SUMMER				"FALL"				WINTER

Rain or hail diurnally, beginning in mid morning, ending in late afternoon or continuing into the night. Cloud cover most of the night | No rain, few or no clouds

Intense solar radiation in early morning | Intense solar radiation all day

Diurnal temperatures cool (about 12°C) | Diurnal shade temperatures cool (about 12°C); black body temperatures in sun > 50°C

Minimum nocturnal temperatures close to 0°C (about -2°C) | Minimum nocturnal temperatures usually considerably below 0°C, often close to -15°C

Diurnal relative humidities variable (50% to 100%); early morning dew or frost | Diurnal relative humidities consistently low (≤ 50%); no dew or frost

Winds unpredictable or none | Strong afternoon winds

*Data compiled from Bowman (1916), Weberbauer (1945), and my own measurements and observations.

habitation. It is impossible to determine for certain what unburned, ungrazed, or lightly grazed puna vegetation resembled before civilization. However, its physiognomy likely would be similar to that of today because of the climate briefly described in the Introduction.

Climatic seasonality and high elevation result in the environmental characteristics outlined in Table 1. The peak of the rainy season occurs in January or February; that of the dry season, in June or July. In southern Peru, annual variation in average monthly temperatures at 16°S latitude is 4.5°C at Puno (3840 m) and 7.1°C at Vincocaya (4420 m), whereas diurnal temperature variation is much greater. For example, at Vincocaya, diurnal variation is maximal (24.1°C) in August and minimal (14.4°C) in February, the latter figure being twice as great as the annual variation (Knoch, 1930, cited in Weberbauer, 1945). This is unlike the situation in the tropical lowlands, where seasonal and diurnal temperature variations are both small (MacArthur, 1972). I made intensive field observations during two wet seasons (September through December, 1968, and January through March, 1970) and one dry season (June through August, 1970). I made some additional observations at the end of the dry season (December, 1971) in northern Chile. During interim periods I studied captive *O. estella* in the laboratory at the University of California at Berkeley.

Methods of Behavioral Studies on *O. estella*

Methodical searches were conducted periodically throughout each of the four study periods, and the habitat and activities of all hummingbirds seen were recorded. An effort was made to examine all habitat types available in the vicinity: open plains, hillsides, gorges with running streams, and dry gorges. Intensive observations were made on selected individuals discovered during the searches. Table 2 shows the distribution of my time into searching periods and actual data collection periods. In addition, an approximately equal total time was spent observing hummingbirds prior to intensive data collection.

TABLE 2
Distribution of Intensive Observation Hours in the Field

Period	Methodical searching	Data collection
1. Sept 1 – Dec 17, 1968	51.0	175.5
2. Jan 15 – Ap 1, 1970	44.0	167.0
3. June 3 – Aug 10, 1970	47.0	102.5
4. Dec 12-17, 1971	10.0	14.0
Total hours	152.0	459.0

In Period 3 (winter), half of the searching time was spent hunting for roosting hummingbirds nocturnally by flashlight in a variety of rock types and vegetation. In the breeding seasons (Periods 1, 2, and 4) about 80 percent of the searching was done diurnally.

My presence did not seem to affect most birds' behavior either at night or in the day. Two particularly nervous nesting females were definitely bothered by my presence during the day; in one case I abandoned regular observation; in the other I was able to make observations from a blind of vegetation about 50 m away. At night, occasionally a roosting hummingbird would flush because of the light and noise disturbances. This almost always occurred in caves or buildings where the light was reflected from many angles. However, flushes were rare, especially during the winter when essentially all birds were torpid and I was making my most critical nocturnal observations.

O. estella was difficult to mist net: these birds nest and roost in pitch-dark caves on occasion (Pearson, 1953; Dorst, 1962) and could conceivably have more acute sensory apparatus than most diurnal birds. As a result, I resorted to capturing roosting birds by night in order to mark individuals with a numbered adhesive band on one leg. This allowed me to identify nocturnal recaptures and follow the roost sites of individuals but was not adequate marking for identification of individuals during the day. Diurnal field identification of individuals was most critical for the observations on territoriality. Most of these observations were done on nesting females. The nest therefore was the basis for field identification of individuals, since a female whose actions centered about a given nest was thereby automatically identified. Furthermore, studies on paint-marked hummingbirds have shown that they have individually characteristic flight paths and perch sites and that these are often so specific that they can be used to identify individuals (Stiles, 1973). This technique was easily employed with *O. estella.* In the studies on territoriality in the nonbreeding season, either an individual's actions could be followed most of the time so that there was no doubt as to its identity, or else sex and behavior were used as a marker. The latter was possible in the observations on territories in *Eucalyptus.*

At the end of study periods 1, 2, and 3, I collected live birds for transportation to laboratory facilities in California. Because I needed a large collection of live individuals for an adequate number to survive the transportation (Carpenter, 1972), and because every live individual detected in the field was a potential captive, I was unable to collect individuals methodically for crop-content analysis. Information on food came from those few individuals that I did shoot, from accident victims, from nestlings whose crop contents actually can be seen through the thin skin, from faecal remains (insect parts went completely through the alimentary canal), and from observations of feeding individuals.

Morphological Adaptations

I. SIZE AND COLOR

Oreotrochilus estella estella is sexually dimorphic in both color and size. The following description of plumage characteristics is based on thirteen males and twenty-five females sexed by dissection. Five of the males and three of the females were known to be nestlings or recent fledglings. The dorsal coloration of all individuals of this subspecies was dull olive grey. The males possessed an iridescent emerald green throat. The white belly of the males was divided longitudinally by a chestnut brown stripe. Three of the five pairs of rectrices of the males were largely white. The females exhibited considerable variation in throat pattern and color. The palest throat was dirty-white with hints of brownish streaks. The brightest female throat had large iridescent green spots. The breast and abdomen were always the same off-white as the throat background. No females possessed the chestnut belly stripe. Most of the rectrices of the females are whitish at the base and tip, with a dark bluish band or blotch centrally. The sexes are easily distinguished in the field because the ventral side of the female in flight appears much less white than that of the male.

The sexes in the young were easily distinguished as soon as the nestlings sprouted their feathers. The young females were indistinguishable by plumage from adult females. The young males possessed a dark green throat with some iridescent feathers immediately beneath the lower mandible: contrary to the description in Dorst (1962), the entire tip of all throat feathers is green so that there is no whitish background as in the females. The newly sprouted belly feathers of the young males already exhibited the chestnut stripe. Their other breast and belly feathers were off-white. The nestling or fledgling male's tail was similar to that of the adult male. A fledgling male could be distinguished from an adult male in the field, but only with great care. Within two months after fledging, the young males developed full adult male plumage (data from two captive males). Since the last fledgings occurred by April (see also Dorst, 1962), the young males probably began the winter in full adult plumage. In fact, all males I saw in the winter were in adult plumage.

O. estella averaged 8.4 gm (N = 24). The mean male weight was 8.8 gm (N = 13), the mean female weight was 8.0 gm (N = 11); the difference was statistically significant (p <.02). I compiled weights of 166 species of hummingbirds from specimens in the Museum of Vertebrate Zoology and from Greenewalt (1960b) for species not represented in the Museum collection; only 7 percent of these equaled or exceeded the weight of *O. estella* (Fig. 3).

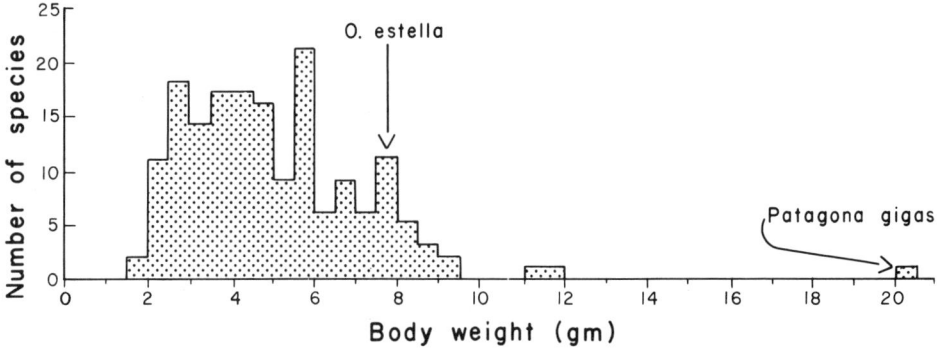

Fig. 3. Size distribution of 166 species of hummingbirds. Data from Greenewalt (1960b, 43 species) and Museum of Vertebrate Zoology specimens (123 species).

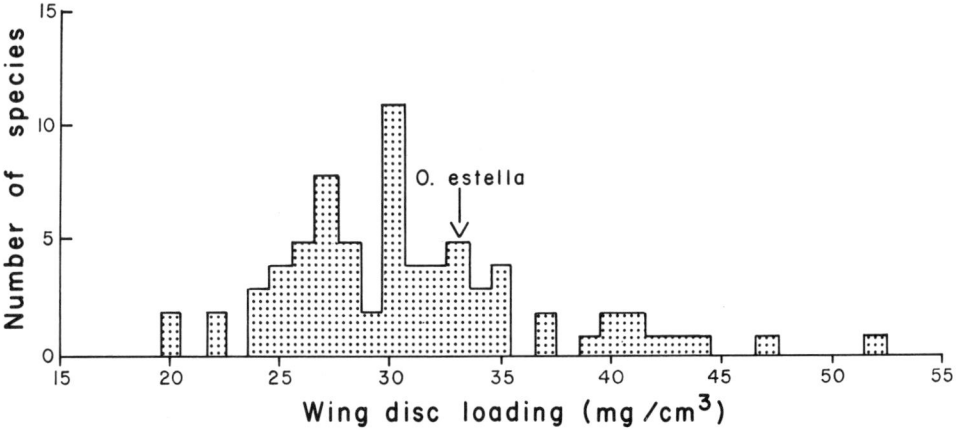

Fig. 4. Distribution of wing disc loading in 74 species of hummingbirds. Data calculated from data in Greenewalt (1960b, 68 species) and from measurements of Museum of Vertebrate Zoology specimens (6 species).

TABLE 3

Tarsus and Toenail Measurements on Specimens in Museum of Vertebrate Zoology, Berkeley, California

Species (N)	Weight (gm)	Tarsus length (mm)	Tarsus % variation	Hallux Nail length (mm)	Hallux Nail % variation
High Andean Species					
Oreotrochilus estella (14)	8.0	0.76 ± .015	1	0.52 ± .01	2
Chalcostigma stanleyi (4)	5.9	0.73 ± .03	4	0.51 ± .01	2
Oxypogon guerinii (1)	5	0.71	--	0.53	--
Other Species					
Coeligena coeligena (6)	6.8	0.42 ± .005	1	0.32 ± .01	3
Anthracothorax nigricollis (6)	7.3	0.40 ± .01	2.5	0.25 ± .01	4
Lampornis clemenciae (6)	7.4	0.57 ± .02	3.5	0.37 ± .015	4
Colibri coruscans (6)	7.6	0.51 ± .005	1	0.27 ± .01	4
Aglaeactis cupripennis (6)	8.0	0.72 ± .02	3	0.44 ± .005	1
Lamprolaima rhami (6)	8.8	0.55 ± .02	4	0.37 ± .004	1
Heliomaster constantii (1)	7.4	0.55	--	0.29	--
Heliodoxa rubinoides (1)	7.8	0.65	--	0.33	--
Eugenes fulgens (1)	7.9	0.55	--	0.31	--
Boissonneaua flavescens (1)	8.6	0.66	--	0.36	--
Campylopterus hemileucurus (1)	8.6	0.67	--	0.28	--
Florisuga mellivora (1)	9	0.46	--	0.22	--

Values given are mean ± one standard deviation

There was no statistical sexual difference in bill length: bills of males averaged 19.8 mm (N = 7); of females, 19.2 mm (N = 13). Upon fledging, the young had attained full body weight but the bill was 20 to 30 percent shorter than that of an adult (14-16 mm; N = 6).

Also using Greenewalt's (1960b) data on 68 species, supplemented by my own measurements with dial calipers on 6 species, I obtained wing length measurements on 74 species for which body weight was also known. From these data, an index called wing disc loading (Epting and Casey, 1973) can be calculated which is directly related to the energetic cost of hovering. Figure 4 shows the distribution of wing disc loading in these hummingbirds. The value for *O. estella* is not statistically different from the mean of other hummingbirds; male and female *O. estella* do not differ in wing loading. The significance of wing disc loading will become clear in the discussion on energetics.

One aspect of size peculiar to all *Oreotrochilus* species is large, strong feet. The strength of the feet is quite apparent when one handles a live bird. Birds with strong feet, such as ground dwellers, usually have a long tarsus and a long opposing toe and nail (hallux). I made foot measurements of male and female *O. estella* and of similar-size hummingbirds in the Museum collection with dial calipers (Table 3). A one-sided t-test was used to compare the set of measurements for *O. estella* with that for non-Andean hummingbirds. This test is valid if the variances within species are all similar; Table 3 shows that they are similar and small (1-4 percent) in those species represented by more than one measurement, indicating that these morphological characteristics are conservative in nature. Both tarsus and hallux are significantly longer ($p < .001$ for both) in *O. estella* than in the other non-Andean species. The other two species of high Andean hummingbirds, *Chalcostigma stanleyi* and *Oxypogon guerinii*, have foot measurements similar to those of *O. estella*.

II. DISCUSSION: ADAPTIVE VALUES OF SIZE AND COLOR

The dull dorsal coloration of *O. estella estella,* unusual in the typically bright green trochilids, is such that the birds blend well into their bleak habitat of rocks and grass. Blending of dorsal coloration with the habitat has been noted in other hummingbird species (Pitelka, 1951). It is conceivable that individuals of *O. estella* occasionally succumb to predation by raptorial birds and that this would be adequate selection pressure for cryptic coloration. Of five species of raptors inhabiting the puna (*Buteo polyosoma, B. poecilochrous, Circus cinereus, Falco sparverius,* and *F. femoralis* : Koepcke, 1964, Johnson, 1965), I saw three commonly on my study sites. These are predators that have color vision and possibly the speed to capture an elusive hummingbird. If in fact there is selection pressure through predation for cyptic coloration, one would expect that the dorsal color of *Oreotrochilus* would become more typically green in forms living in greener páramo to the north. In fact, both *O. estella stolzmanni* in northern Peru and *O. chimborazo* in Ecuador have much brighter and greener dorsal plumage than do *O. estella estella, O. adela,* or *O. leucopleurus* — all puna inhabitants (de Schauensee, 1970; Museum of Vertebrate Zoology specimens).

The prevailing colors in the habitat also may have played a role in the color evolved for display in the male gorget. Because the emerald green contrasts well with the yellows and browns of the habitat, it may lend a more striking aspect to the gorget when displayed. It is noteworthy that *O. chimborazo* in Equadorian páramo is the only *Oreotrochilus* form that has a violet head and throat — green presumably would offer less contrast in that environment.

The juvenile males of most hummingbirds require about a year to acquire full adult plumage (Bent, 1940). *O. estella* males are precocious in this respect. Unfortunately, I have no longevity data to help explain possible forces acting to produce such precociousness. However, population size plummets over the winter without seeming to be replenished by immigration at the beginning of the breeding season (present study), implying high winter mortality. If this is true, there would be selection pressure for the young to breed in their first year (Gadgil and Bossert, 1970), before undergoing the risks of winter. This would be feasible for young produced early in the long (seven month) breeding season. Such a situation would in turn place selection pressure on young males to develop their breeding colors quickly. In addition, because the male apparently breeds opportunistically, there would be selection pressure for first-year males to begin the next breeding season already possessing full adult plumage. Yet moult is likely to be energetically unfeasible in the winter under natural conditions. Thus, it again is preferable for a young male to begin the winter in full adult plumage.

Size is undoubtedly an important adaptive trait (McNab, 1971; see Hainsworth and Wolf, 1972, for a discussion of body-size effects on foraging efficiency). If the aberrantly large *Patagona gigas* is discounted, hummingbirds range in size from 2 to 12 gm, most falling in the 2 to 6 gm range (Fig. 3). The 8 gm *O. estella* is unusually large in comparison. In the larger species of hummingbirds (> 4 gm), males are larger than females (Lasiewski and Lasiewski, 1967). This is true for most nonraptorial birds, is true for *O. estella*, and is traditionally explained by sexual selection favoring territorially successful individuals. This may be an inadequate explanation for the size dimorphism in *O. estella*, however, because the males do not aggressively defend territories (see section on territoriality). Alternative explanations may be that (1) large size makes for a more striking courtship display or (2) the males require an advantage in efficient linear flight, which is conferred by larger size. An analysis of the latter is developed in more detail in the section on energetics.

In any event, smaller size in the females may give them a certain advantage during seasons of food shortage. There is a season of food shortage for hummingbirds wherever there is seasonality in the blooming of nectar-producing plants — and this occurs almost everywhere, even in the lowland tropics (Stiles and Wolf, 1970). Survival throughout a long period when food is scarce is more likely if the total energy demands of the bird are lower (cf. Pough, 1973). In general, the smaller the bird, the less total energy it requires, the smaller the foraging area it must exploit (present study; Stiles and Wolf, 1970), and the greater its probability of surviving an entire season of food sparseness.

In the smaller species of hummingbirds (< 4 gm), however, exactly reverse sexual dimorphism occurs, with males being smaller than females (Lasiewski and Lasiewski, 1967). Why has sexual selection "failed" in these cases? The metabolic rate of the smaller species is so fast that they can starve to death in a matter of just a few hours. Ecologically, this means that a storm severe enough to prevent feeding for a day can cause mortality, depending upon body size. This is of particular importance to a female feeding and incubating young, because the demands on her energy are high and she apparently resists entering nocturnal torpor (Carpenter, 1974; Howell and Dawson, 1954; Calder, 1971), although she may go torpid in extreme emergencies (Calder and Booser, 1973). If these stringent requirements of the females are coupled with any selection for resource partitioning between sexes, then among the small species, females should tend to be larger than males. This same argument can be applied to explain the large size of hummingbirds in general on the altiplano. Severe weather conditions often arise that potentially prevent feeding or reduce the amount of food available to the hummingbirds. Sudden hailstorms and heavy rains occur in the summer breeding season and may last for several hours. Such sudden, temporary emergencies might prove disastrous for a very small hummingbird with typically fast metabolic rate and low energy reserves. Temporary emergencies should select for relatively large size in hummingbirds that frequent the altiplano, but this conflicts with the selection pressure for small size caused by extended periods of food shortage. The fact that the three species occurring in my study areas are all large — *O. estella*; *Colibri coruscans*, averaging 7.7 gm (N = 6); and *Patagona gigas*, averaging 20.3 gm (N = 14) — indicates that short-term emergencies, and possibly other considerations such as migration (McNab, 1971), have acted as the stronger selection pressures on high Andean hummingbirds, along with selection pressures relating to efficiency of linear flight.

Wolf (1969) predicted that if both sexes use and defend territories for the same food plant species during periods of food shortage, there should be selection for similar bill lengths. He tabulated data on five resident species in which females hold nonbreeding feeding territories and five resident species in which they do not, and found support for his hypothesis. *O. estella* supports his prediction also, as the sexes both use the same food plants in the winter (present study) and possess almost identical bill lengths in spite of significant differences in weight.

The final aspect of size to discuss here is perhaps the most significant and certainly the least speculative. This is the large foot size of *O. estella*. The perching, roosting, and feeding behavior of *O. estella* are all affected by the large foot size and will be discussed in detail in a later section. To summarize, the birds roost in caves and rocky areas, and they often perch on and feed from the ground. Similar roosting behavior has been noted in *O. chimborazo* (French and Hodges, 1959) and probably also occurs in *O. leucopleurus* since this species also is saxicolous (Johnson, 1967), that is, associated with rocks. This is a unique adaptive strategy within hummingbirds — no other genus that I know has been reported to roost clinging to cave walls and to rocks. To cling vertically or upside down to rock surfaces requires a strong grip: thus, selection pressure for stronger, larger feet than is usual in hummingbirds. Other selection pressures undoubtedly acted simultaneously to increase the size of *Oreotrochilus* feet, such as feeding while perched on the ground or on branches. Two other Andean genera, *Chalcostigma* and *Oxypogon*, also have large feet (Table 2). These species are known to ground feed (Ruschi, 1961b, 1967; Vuilleumier, 1966); there is some evidence that they may roost in rocky areas (Ruschi, 1961a). *O. estella* usually perch in front of or on the flowers from which they feed, and are rarely seen hover feeding (see next section). These environmental conditions — rocky shelters, lack of robust vegetation, occurrence of food near the ground — and the energy saved by perch feeding (Snow and Snow, 1971; Hainsworth and Wolf, 1972; present study) all should select for large, strong feet in a species whose way of life must necessarily be more terrestrial and less arboreal than in most trochilids. An apparent exception is *Colibri coruscans*, which successfully breeds on the altiplano where there are *Polylepis* or *Eucalyptus* trees and has typically small feet (Table 3). However, it roosts in vegetation, hover feeds, and does not remain in residence during the winter. Thus, it seems probable that winter conditions were those that most strenuously selected for large feet in *Oreotrochilus*. Specifically, I think that the crucial role of cave roosting in the winter, combined with the energetic advantages of perch feeding, especially important during the energy-limited winter, were the primary selection forces. The large feet of *Oxypogon* and *Chalcostigma* suggest that they also may remain resident at high elevation during the winter.

Behavioral Adaptations: Foraging and Roosting

I. GROUND- AND ROCK-DWELLING HABITS

Feeding Techniques

Individuals of *O. estella* spent some of their foraging time on the ground. They gleaned from rock surfaces and crevices while perched on the rocks, even if the surface was vertical or overhanging. They moved about the rocks with great agility, clinging to the surfaces with their strong feet and using their tail as a brace. They also gleaned from the bare ground between clumps of bunchgrass, possibly to pick up the beetles or ants that occur there or to pick up soil particles, perhaps where the calcium content was high (Verbeek, 1971). The birds often hopped rather than flew from one foraging spot to the next. The hopping was slightly awkward, with the wings held a fraction open and sometimes fluttering slightly.

This species also preferred to perch while foraging from flowers with available landing platforms (Fig. 5). The main native plant species used were orange flowered *Cajophora* spp (Loasaceae), a brilliant, red flowered cactus (*Echinopsis*?), and a yellow flowered *Opuntia* (Cactaceae), red or white *Bomarea dulcis* (Amaryllidaceae), and orange *Chuquiraga spinosa* (Compositae, tribe Mutisieae). Some of these plants are shown in Plates 1 and 2. The cacti and *Cajophora* grow close to the ground and the birds could amost always perch on the ground or on the plant to feed. Once I watched a female approach a *Cajophora* flower that was about six inches above the ground: while hovering she inserted her bill into the cuplike flower, settled vertically to the ground pulling the flower down with her bill, and fed sequentially from the five nectaries while perched on the ground. *Bomarea dulcis* plants are long stemmed and have vertically hanging red or white flowers — these were the only flowers at which *O. estella* consistently hovered.

I never saw *Chuquiraga* used during the breeding season although Dorst (1962) did. During my winter studies it was essentially the only native hummingbird flower that bloomed and provided *O. estella* with an important winter food source. The birds invariably perched on the stems or involucres of the inflorescences while feeding. Small amounts of nectar are secreted by *Chuquiraga* (D. Bradford and F. R. Hainsworth, pers. comm.), but copious quantities of pollen are extruded. Individuals of *O. estella* that have been feeding on *C. spinosa* are coated with the bright orange pollen on the forehead and chin, and moistly caked pollen occurs in the corners of the mandibles (Fig. 6). These plants apparently provide pollen as food for the hummingbirds (observations by D'Orbigny, reported in Gould, 1861), which is much higher in proteins than are nectars (Percival, 1965; Baker and Baker, 1973). The small amounts of nectar secreted by *Chuquiraga* may serve to aid in amino acid extraction from the pollen (see Gilbert, 1972). Pollen was found in the five gut analyses performed on *O. estella* in Bolivia by Langner (1973) in the winter, but was not identified taxonomically.

The proportion of hover feeding to perch feeding at flowers was less in the winter than in the summer breeding season (Fig. 5). The absolute amount of hovering shown in the winter in Figure 5 is high because of my many hours of observation of *Eucalyptus*. No hovering and very little flycatching occurred in *Chuquiraga* areas, even though insect availabilities in the *Eucalyptus* area (garden) and the *Chuquiraga* areas (bushy gorges) were comparable (Fig. 7c).

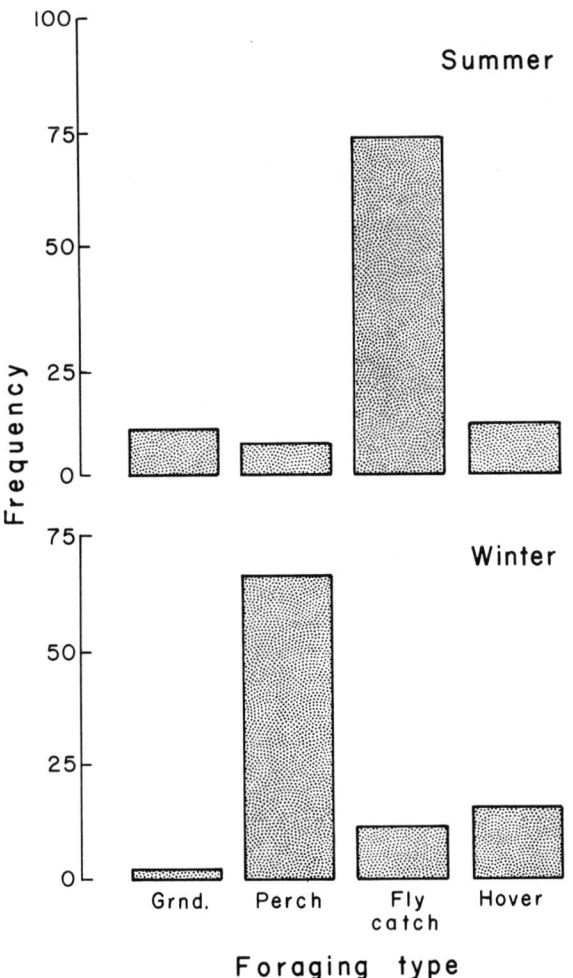

Fig. 5. Seasonal changes in frequency of types of feeding behavior. Histogram showing the proportion of bouts of different types of feeding behavior in the summer (N = 165) and winter (N = 94). Feeding types are arranged along the abscissa in order of increasing energetic cost: ground feeding < perch feeding at flowers < flycatching < hover feeding at flowers. Hovering is more costly than linear flight (Tucker, 1968; Pennycuick, 1968; 1969) and flycatching is largely linear. An uninterrupted bout of one of the types of feeding was counted as one bout regardless of the number of flowers probed or the number of fly-catching sorties. In the winter, 94 percent of the flycatching and 93 percent of the hover feeding occurred in *Eucalyptus* areas, very little occurring in native habitat with *Chuquiraga*. Almost all observations in the summer involved females; observations in the winter involved both sexes, between which no difference in behavior was apparent.

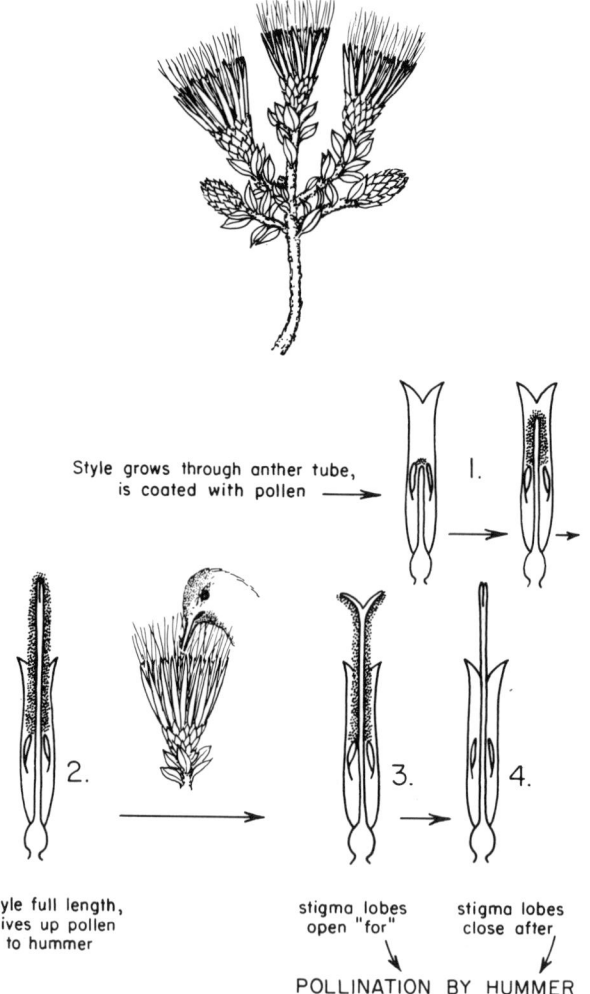

Fig. 6. Pollination of *Chuquiraga spinosa*. At the top of the figure is a terminal branch of *Chuquiraga spinosa* showing three inflorescences and exerted styles; 3/4 natural size. The rest of the figure shows the development and pollination of a single floret 2 x natural size (except for the insert between stages 2 and 3). Stippling on the hummingbird in the insert indicates areas of pollen occurrence on the forehead and chin and of pollen conglomeration in the corner of the mandible. *Chuquiraga spinosa* possesses only tubular florets. Each floret is protandrous, the pollen being shed as the style grows through the fused anther tube situated midway between the base and top of the corolla. The style continues to grow upwards, pulling the pollen with it so that the style and inside of the corolla tube are coated with pollen. Selfing is avoided because the lobes of the stigma do not open until the style has lifted them far above the anther and corolla tubes.

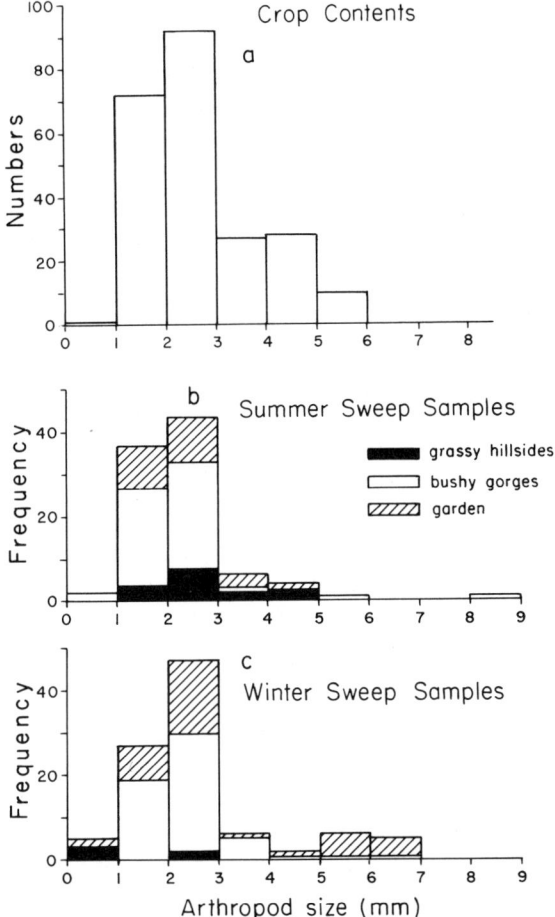

Fig. 7. The insect food of *O. estella*.

a. Numerical distribution of the sizes of insect food in *O. estella* in the summer breeding season. Data from crops of three individuals and excreta from four individuals.

b. Frequency distribution of the sizes of arthropods captured by sweep netting in three areas occupied by *O. estella* in the summer breeding season (N = 248 arthropods). Each of the three areas was swept the same number of times under the same weather conditions, so that relative abundances in the areas are indicated by the shadings of the histogram bars.

c. Frequency distribution of the sizes of arthropods captured in the winter by sweep netting the same number of times in the same three areas under similar weather conditions as in b (N = 48).

Both males and females flycaught in the summer. Males perched on the open hillsides and hawked poorwill style from the ground. Females in the rocky gorges usually used rocks from which to flycatch. However, where *Polylepis* trees were available, their branches also were used as flycatching perches in more typical hummingbird style, probably not only because they offered good vantage points but also because many small insects are attracted to them for shelter (Dorst, 1962). These flycatching techniques probably used more energy than did gleaning insects from surfaces while perched or hopping.

I censused aerial insects by sweep netting, pacing at a constant rate to make censuses comparable. I swept areas where I saw hummingbirds flycatching and also control areas without hummingbirds. I censused under various climatic conditions but, to make cross-seasonal comparisons in Figure 7, I only included samples from sunny summer periods with ambient temperatures and solar radiation similar to winter periods. From analysis of three crops and the chitinous remains found in the black tarry part of the excreta of four individuals, I determined that the birds were taking dipterans from 1.0 to 6.0 mm in length. They were therefore taking generally items in the same proportions in which they were available, although there was undoubtedly some selection perhaps based on size and/or distastefulness. The census samples, for example, did not reveal three large insect species that I collected at other times: a large orange bumblebee, a wasp 1 cm long, and a nymphalid butterfly.

Observations of a 20-day-old nestling in February showed that a fluid, presumably nectar, was the sole food fed to the young early in the morning. The insect component increased until by mid-afternoon the crop was packed with insects.

Roosting

Plates 3 and 4 show typical nocturnal roosts of this species. Invariably, both sexes roosted in rocky areas or buildings. As described under morphological adaptations, the birds clung to rocks, ceilings, and walls with their large feet and claws, using the tail as a brace just as they did while gleaning (Pearson, 1953). They clung to vertical surfaces head up, and to the underside of overhangs with their bodies inverted and horizontal. Out of fourteen summer and twenty-five winter roost sites, only one was occupied by a hummingbird perched on top of a horizontal surface. Many species in other avian families, especially flycatchers and furnariids, used the horizontal rock surfaces for roosting (see also Pearson, 1953).

There was a distinct change in the character of the roost sites as winter approached. Summer roost sites were in relatively exposed situations: a rock facing the center of a gorge, an interior wall of a building, the underside of a ledge that jutted out only a few inches from a rock wall. The positions of the birds within the fourteen summer roosts ranged from 1 to 7 m above ground, averaging 1.5 m above ground. Minimum ambient temperatures in these sites were about 5 to 8°C above the outside temperatures (Fig. 8). In June the birds began to abandon their summer roosts. Four individuals that I studied alternated between two roost sites; all eventually abandoned the first one, which had been the summer site. Winter roosts were more enclosed. Out of twenty-five winter sites discovered, eighteen were in caves, four inside abandoned, well-insulated buildings, and three in old nests in shelters. In cave roosts the birds were usually surrounded by rock on several sides, often in crevices and oblong holes scarcely larger than their bodies. These sites ranged from 0.6 to 7 m above ground, averaging 1 m above ground. I measured ambient temperatures within the crevice microhabitats while the birds occupied the roosts. Minimum temperatures ranged from 1 to 8°C, averaging 5°C; this was as much as 15°C above minimum ambient temperature outside the caves or buildings.

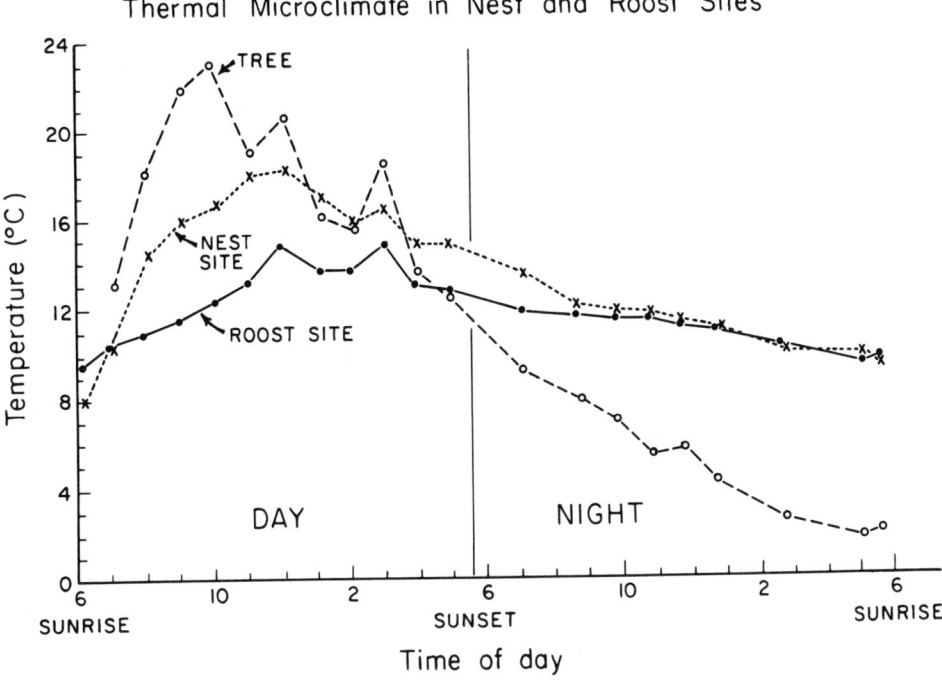

Fig. 8. Thermal microclimate in nest and roost sites. Hourly temperatures were recorded simultaneously during one 24-hr summer period in a roost site and near (15 cm from) an occupied nest. The "tree" site was under a branch of *Polylepis* situated in the open center of the gorge. General location is shown in Plate 3.

I observed one female roosting several nights in a barn in June. One night in late June the temperature was lower than usual and there was a strong wind which entered the barn's open windows. I noticed that the wind ruffled the roosting female's feathers. To my knowledge, she survived the night, yet I never saw her again in that roost. There were four other individuals roosting in more protected parts of the barn. Three of them retained those roost sites throughout the rest of the winter. The observation on the wind-blown female raised the question of what cue or cues prompt a hummingbird to seek a new roost site. The obvious cue one imagines is ambient temperature: if the roost temperature falls below a physiologically critical level (5-7°C in this species: Carpenter, 1974), the bird should be able to sense this, even if torpid, and should react by seeking a more protected site for the future. To see if temperature did affect roost habits, I conducted an experiment in the laboratory on thirteen individuals placed in four 0.6 x 0.5 x 0.5 m cages made of cardboard boxes with three of the four walls replaced by mesh tulle to which the birds could easily cling. A 0.8 m length of 3/16" dowelling served as a horizontal perch. There were rough edges on the ceilings to which the birds also could cling. I had held captive birds in such cages in Peru both in the summer and winter and had noticed that summer birds always roosted on the dowelling or the tulle walls, whereas winter birds tended to settle in the four upper corners and on the ceiling. I kept captive birds in the laboratory in California at 15°C in the day and 10°C at night. To test if a drop in temperature below 5°C cues roost change, I placed two cages with six individuals in a room at 5°C and the other two boxes with seven individuals at 0°C. Temperature was controlled to ±1°C. The birds remained in these rooms for three days on a 12-hr photoperiod and their roosting positions within the cages were noted each night. The results are in Table 4. The birds tended to respond after just one night at the lower temperature by seeking more enclosed roost sites.

TABLE 4
Change of Perch Site with Change in Temperature

	On perch 5°C 0°C	On tulle walls 5°C 0°C	In corners or on ceiling 5°C 0°C
Night 1	2 3	4 4	0 0
Night 2	2 0	4 3	0 4
Night 3	2 0	4 3	0 4

II. DISCUSSION: ADAPTIVENESS AND COMPARATIVE ASPECTS OF FORAGING AND ROOSTING BEHAVIOR

The adaptiveness and unique nature of the saxicolous and ground habits of *O. estella* can hardly be overemphasized. Almost all other known species of hummingbirds are chiefly arboreal, although they occasionally descend to the ground to pick up insects (Bent, 1940) or particles of earth (Verbeek, 1971). Their food, water, roost sites, and nesting material all occur generally above ground and among or on the leaves and twigs of bushes and trees. Because the vegetation structure is so different on the altiplano, birds in general must become more terrestrial. The vegetation structure combined with the fact that climatic conditions differ from those of more lowland areas forces small birds to seek nocturnal shelter among rocks or else migrate to lower elevations in the winter. *O. estella* is the most abundant hummingbird species in the puna of southern Peru (Dorst, 1962; personal observation). *Colibri coruscans* is the only other species that occurs in noticeable numbers. It not only emigrates in the winter, but is also restricted in summer to areas with trees or *Polylepis* shrubs. Its populations are small compared to those of *O. estella* and are apparently subject to large fluctuations (Dorst, 1962).

The development of large, strong feet in *Oreotrochilus* was probably the major evolutionary change that opened up an entirely new and successful way of life for these hummingbirds. All facets of their lives — feeding, perching, bathing, and roosting — can be done independently of the occurrence of most vegetation. Not surprisingly, the only other hummingbird genera known to have extensive ground habits are *Oxypogon* in the Venezuelan Andes and *Chalcostigma* in the Ecuadorian Andes (Ruschi, 1961b; 1967).

Their strong feet have freed *O. estella* not only from most vegetation requirements but also from the necessity of costly hovering. Hovering requires more work at high altitude than at sea level because the air is less dense and gives less lift (Pennycuick, 1969). At 4000 m the power required to hover is increased: if calculated by a method from Pennycuick (1969), the increase is 25 percent; however, Berger (1974) actually measured about a 10 percent increase at 4000 m. Whereas hovering is a tremendous advantage to hummingbirds in vegetated areas because it increases access to flowers, insects, and nesting materials, hovering is probably an energetic liability at sparsely vegetated high altitudes. The preponderance of perch feeding in *O. estella,* especially in the winter, is then reasonable. Significantly, when and where more energy is available — i.e., during the summer blooming season and in winter-blooming *Eucalyptus* — *O. estella* hover feeds more frequently. Furthermore, more hovering occurs in *Eucalyptus* than in *Chuquiraga* in spite of the fact that the large, tough twigs and flowers of the former offer potential landing platforms.

Because these birds have retained the ability to hover feed and to perch on twigs when available, the new way of life provided by their stronger feet is that of a generalist. The birds can exploit typical hummingbird resources in the typical hummingbird manner when these are available, but they also can become terrestrial when necessary. *O. estella* is a saxicoline specialist when roosting and nesting, however. These activities are performed in rocky areas even when the closest competitor, *Colibri coruscans,* is absent.

A coevolutionary pollination relationship is suggested for *O. estella* and *Chuquiraga spinosa* (Fig. 6; see Carpenter, 1972). *C. spinosa* possesses the red color and adhesive pollen characteristic of bird-pollinated flowers (Grant and Grant, 1968). It was the only native hummingbird flower that bloomed in numbers during the winter at my study sites. In addition the peak of blooming of this and certain other similar species of *Chuquiraga* occurs in the winter (Weberbauer, 1945). It is likely that without *C. spinosa, O. estella* would be an altitudinal migrant like *Colibri* and would not have evolved the adaptations that enable its survival over the winter. That the plants provide highly proteinaceous pollen to the birds during their energy-limited season is probably one reason why the birds do not perform costly flycatching in the winter (Fig. 5) in spite of at least occasional insect availability (arthropods were 20 percent as abundant in the winter as in the summer — see captions to Fig. 7). They do not need to flycatch because their protein requirements are supplied by the pollen. Pollen feeding by birds has been reported sporadically (one or two cases) in several North American hummingbirds (see Bent, 1940), has been observed in one Central American species (R. Colwell, pers. comm.), and is of major importance to nectar-feeding lorikeets in Australia (Churchill and Christensen, 1970).

Perch feeding at *C. spinosa* is facilitated by the large, rough involucres to which the birds easily cling while feeding. This is reminiscent of the landing platforms of many insect-pollinated flowers which also yield their pollinators little energy reward but provide them with an energy-saving perch instead (Heinrich and Raven, 1972). Some other bird plants provide landing platforms for the nonhovering African sunbirds (Skead, 1967; Wolf, pers. comm.).

In return, *C. spinosa* obtains a pollinator that is more dependable than wind or insects (Cruden, 1972) and is able to avoid competition for that pollinator (Levin and Anderson, 1970) by blooming when no other hummingbird flowers bloom. Stiles (1973) suggested that the most tightly coevolved relationships with birds might be expected in plants that bloom during the energy-limited season for the birds: then the ratio of nectar to birds is lowest so that the probability of a plant being visited is highest, and the pollinator is therefore dependable and predictable. The relationship of *O. estella* with *C. spinosa* fits this hypothesis. In addition, other *Chuquiraga* species seem to be distributed with other *Oreotrochilus* species, the reddish species with long corollas occurring only where some form of *Oreotrochilus* also occurs (Carpenter, 1972).

Many tropical hummingbirds probably are selective in the size of the insects they take merely because there is a great size range of insects available in the lowland tropics (see Schoener, 1971). *O. estella* seems to be nonselective and to take insects in the proportions in which they occur, but a great size range is not available. A more truly nonselective situation exists in frugivores, which do not seem to partition fruit resources. Snow and Snow (1971) have suggested that this is because fruits are similar to each other and thus only a few variations of adaptation to fruit exploitation can be developed. Whether or not this is true for fruit exploitation, it probably does apply to very small aerial insects, and selectivity according to size would not be expected in any event.

Female *O. estella* with young may show food selectivity in another way, however. They apparently feed their young nectar in the early mornings and insects later to give the young easily digested, quick-energy carbohydrates after their long (up to 13 hr) nocturnal fast and a subsequent supply of protein, required for growth and development. Females with young apparently are selecting food types for their young according to the time of day. However, since the diurnal rhythms of nectar and insect availability were not studied, it is possible that the female's pattern merely reflects relative availability of the two food categories. The feeding pattern is obviously adaptive regardless of its proximate causes, and may be even more crucial to normal development of the young at high elevations than it would be to the young of most hummingbirds. It would be interesting to see if the same pattern pertains among lowland hummingbirds.

Nocturnal predation avoidance, competition for sites, and microclimatic advantages are possible selection pressures causing roost specificity of this species. The roost locations make these birds essentially inaccessible to predators. This could be important because this species often becomes torpid at night, in which state individuals are completely helpless. There are not many nocturnal predators on the altiplano: the only snake (*Tachymenis peruviana*) is probably strictly diurnal; owls (*Tyto alba, Bubo virginianus*) probably would not detect an immobile prey item, nor would foxes (*Dusicyon culpaeus*) or cats (*Felis colocolo*), although these latter might take a small bird roosting on the ground. The most likely predator on birds roosting at night in vegetation or rocky areas is probably the weasel (*Mustela frenata*). Weasels could produce selection pressure against the hummingbirds roosting on top of ledges or in holes. In this regard, Ruschi (1961a) comments on the unusual, cockroach-like odor characterizing the skin of *O. estella*. The odor is powerful and unpleasant and conceivably could render the species distasteful to mammalian predators. On the other hand, the presence of many other species of birds roosting in caves and rocks (Pearson, 1953) may produce some competition for horizontal surfaces and holes; by clinging to vertical walls or ceilings the hummingbirds would avoid such competition.

The microclimatic advantages of such roosting sites are obvious. They are warmer than the surroundings and are probably more humid. They present the possibility of both absorbing reradiated body heat and of rebreathing humid air, since water and heat from the body are not lost as rapidly as they would be to an open sky (Gates, 1962). These factors combine to reduce heat and water losses to the cold, dry air. Water conservation at night possibly may be almost as important during the winter as is energy and heat conservation since this is the dry season as well as the cold season. The fact that the birds are never found far from free water in the winter suggests that they may need free drinking water during the day and that water conservation at night is important. Switching from summer to winter roosts with the onset of lower nocturnal temperatures suggests that reductions in heat and water losses are important factors in roost-site selection. The cue for switching seems to be low temperature. With the onset of winter, the birds probably change roosts until they find one that satisfies their fairly specific requirements (Carpenter, 1974). With the beginning of breeding in the summer, spacing requirements (next section) prevent the concentration of birds in one area, local dispersal occurs, and the relatively mild environmental conditions permit occupancy of less protected sites.

The section to follow on reproduction and the annual cycle will show the evidence for high mortality during the winter, which places a premium on energy-saving adaptations.

Reproductive Adaptations

I. REPRODUCTION

Dorst (1962) treated in detail the nest and nest-site characteristics, courtship, and care and development of the young of *O. estella*. My work corroborates some of the aspects of his work and sheds further light on others. I also have some additional material that should be added to the picture of breeding adaptations in this species.

There is a distinct seasonality to the breeding of *O. estella* in southern Peru (Fig. 9). The earliest signs of nesting that I witnessed occurred August 3, 1970, when a female began adding to an old nest in a barn situated near a luxuriant garden. I was unable to follow the fate of this nest. The earliest nesting behavior that I was able to follow to completion began probably in late August, 1968: on September 4 I found a female building on the small beginnings of a nest under a rocky overhang in a small gorge. The only plants in bloom in the immediate area at that time were cacti. Egglaying occurred on September 20, hatching on October 11, and fledging from November 2 to 6. Blooming of *Cajophora* began on September 20 and the first steady rains came on September 25. Both in 1968 and in 1970, then, the earliest nesters began work considerably before the first rains, but not so early that care of the young began before the first flush of blossoms.

Figure 9 shows the increase of number of clutches laid with respect to time and the rainy season in 1968 and 1970. Measured by laying of clutches, the peak of the breeding season occurred in January, which is within a month of the peak of the rainy season. The last fledglings were out of the nests by early April in 1970. No nesting occurred during the peak of the dry winter season (1970 data).

The cycle of population size estimated by relative changes in numbers of hummingbird individuals accounted for is shown in Figure 10. Densities of individuals were usually low enough that I could make diurnal estimates of numbers by observing interactions and by knowing territory or home-range locations; these estimates then were compared to the current count of roosting hummingbirds. In general, the two methods of estimating the number of individuals in a given study site at a given time agreed closely. At the end of the winter there was no dramatic influx of individuals into the area but instead numbers built up gradually with the production of young. Since no observations were made in April or

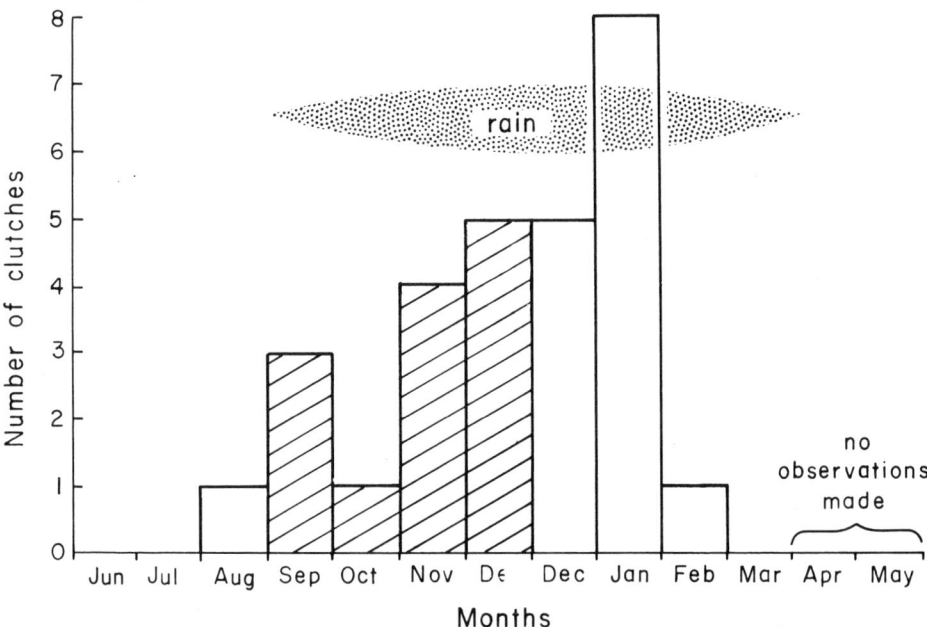

Fig. 9. Breeding season. Histogram of number of clutches laid each month in a given area. Clutches laid in September–December, 1968, are indicated by the cross-hatched bars; open bars represent December–August, 1970. Note that December is represented twice along the monthly axis, once for 1968 and once for 1970. December dates for 1970 were obtained by extrapolation based on the stages at which nests were found in January, 1970. The clutch indicated for August, 1970, was not laid before I left in early August, but the advanced state of nest building suggested that egg laying should occur soon. Approximate intensity of rains is indicated by the relative width of the stippled pattern above the histogram.

May, the decline in numbers of hummingbirds may have been less gradual than is indicated by connecting data points in March with those in June.

Dorst (1962) described in detail the exceptionally large size and thick insulation of *O. estella* nests, and Calder (1973) has shown the thermal advantages of nests to females in another species of montane hummingbird. My work was intended to show the thermal advantages of the nest locations. In studying the characteristics of nest sites, I worked only with occupied nests because hummingbirds are known to abandon a nest without use even after it is completed. Thus, I restricted my observations to nests that were proven to be satisfactory for use. Of 29 occupied nests studied, 3 were in caves, 14 under overhanging rock ledges, 6 inside buildings or archways, 4 under thatched eaves, and 2 under the "skirts" of *Puya raimondi* (Bromeliaceae; Plate 3). Other vegetation types were searched unsuccessfully for nests: *Polylepis, Ribes, Baccharis,* and other shrubs. I am certain that my methodical searches revealed most occupied nests because nesting females are territorial and advertise vocally. They are even easier to detect than are the bright-colored territorial males of North American species because puna vegetation is so open.

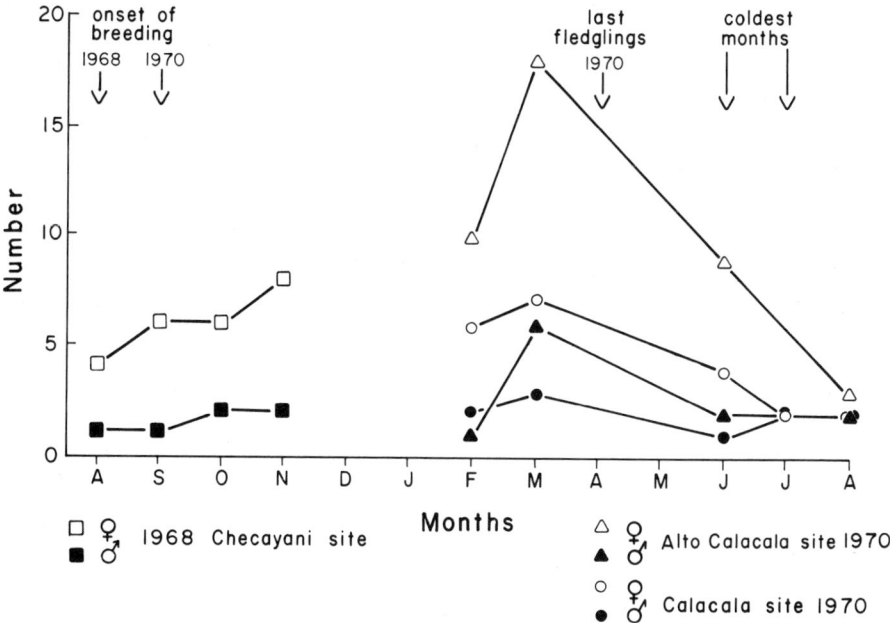

Fig. 10. Population sizes of *O. estella*, estimated by changes in numbers of different individuals accounted for diurnally and in roosts each month in one 1968 study site and two 1970 study sites.

The mean height of the nests above ground was 1.9 m (range: 1.2-3.1 m) and the mean clearance between the lip of the nest and the ceilinglike overhang was 7.1 cm (range: 4.6-10.0 cm). All nests were built so close under overhangs that sun never struck the nest, not even on nests built on east- or west-facing sides of gorges. Of 27 categorizable nests, 8 faced generally east and 4 faced generally west. The others faced north or south. The direction faced was random with respect to the position of the rising or setting sun.

These nest localities offered moderate microclimates for the young and the mother (Fig. 8; see also Dorst, 1962). The mother apparently attempts to thermoregulate throughout incubation and brooding (Carpenter, 1974), so the thermal advantages of the rocky microhabitats are obvious. Buildings offered similar thermal advantages, the minimum ambient temperature rarely falling below 10°C. However, the sites under *Puya* skirts (Plate 3) were less effectively protected against nocturnal cold, although they were equally protected from direct solar radiation, wind, rain, and hail.

Puya sites were probably inferior to typical rocky nest sites in two additional ways: first, *Puya* occurred on open hillsides where hummingbird flowers were scarce and insect densities low; second, there was no adjacent water supply, the nearest water being 1/2 to 1 km distant and access to which required invading other nesting females' territories. Feeding and bathing thus were probably energetically more expensive for the *Puya* females because of greater flight distances between resources and greater likelihood of territorial encounters.

Since *O. estella* females defend combined nesting and feeding territories, the question arises as to whether any females are prevented from breeding by being excluded to marginal or unsuitable habitat. Several pieces of evidence suggested that there was severe competition for a limited number of suitable nest sites in 1968 and 1970.

1. A female that was discovered in the early stages of nest building on September 4, 1968, was often occupied by chasing an invading female from her nesting and feeding territory. The second female had an adjacent defended area of her own up the side of the gorge. Her area included several *Puya raimondi* plants but no rocky areas or vegetation other than grasses and cacti. I periodically checked the *Puya* for an *O. estella* nest but never found one. This secondary female continued her challenges upon the primary female's territory throughout incubation, brooding, and caring for the young. When these young fledged, I collected the fledglings and the primary female disappeared. The next day a new female was building upon the primary female's abandoned nest and advertising her ownership. The secondary female's *Puya* territory was abandoned. Thus, the new female was probably the secondary female. Within a month, she laid her first egg in the nest. This was still before the peak of the breeding season and she would have had ample time to bring off young.

2. *Puya* plants, already suggested to be inferior nest sites, were not used until December, after at least three months of breeding had already been under way and the nearby gorges were filled to nesting capacity.

3. In 1970 when I began my studies in the middle of the breeding season, two situations of semicolonial nesting occurred. These are described in detail under territorial adaptations. Semicolonialism results in many territorial encounters because of the proximity of nests; it also forces the females to feed in areas separated by as much as 1/2 km from their nests. Thus, more energy is probably spent in territorial conflicts and in flying to and from feeding areas. Another probable disadvantage of semicolonialism is interference with fledging. Of three successful nests built close together in one complex rock outcropping, the first to fledge showed a case of fledging interference. The movements of the young *O. estella* took it into the highly defended nest territory of an adjacent neighbor. When the neighbor returned to her nest, she saw the fledgling perched nearby and attacked it vigorously, knocking it off the rock and to the ground. The fledgling remained as though stunned on the ground for several minutes before flying back up to the rock outcrop and eventually returning to its nest. The dangers of such interference to a weak-flying fledgling are obvious.

4. In a barn in mid-January, 1970, two females were discovered incubating two eggs each in nests 10 m apart. The female with more advanced eggs (hatched 4 days sooner) was definitely behaviorally dominant. (She will be referred to as the "dominant" henceforth.) Chases between the two were always initiated by the dominant. The subordinate had apparently begun a previous nest 3 m from that of the dominant and had laid one egg in the nest: at the time of discovery of these two females, the subordinate continually flew from her occupied nest to the abandoned one and attempted to enter the latter but was always chased by the dominant. When she would return to the barn, she would enter by a back window far from the nest of the dominant, and would fly to her incubated nest. After incubating, she would fly hesitatingly toward the abandoned nest and repeat the performance. Within a week she gradually ceased this behavior and concentrated her attention on the incubated nest. At this point I removed the egg from the abandoned nest and

opened it — it was fresh and undeveloped. In reconstructing what apparently happened, I think that the subordinate female first built a nest and laid an egg in it. Before she could lay the second egg the dominant female arrived and was able to displace her. The first female then began a second nest farther away from the dominant. The dominant completed and laid in her nest slightly before the subordinate was able to complete her new nest. This all would have occurred at the peak of the breeding season.

These four incidents reveal competition for nest sites and perhaps decreased nest-site selectivity during the peak of the breeding season. It remains unclear whether potentially breeding females are ever actually prevented from breeding but they may be delayed in breeding or forced to breed in marginal habitat.

Dorst (1962) commented on the relatively long incubation and nestling periods of *O. estella*. The few nests I followed from egg-laying time to hatching confirmed his figure of 20 days for incubation. Most of the nests I followed from hatching to fledging required about 38 days, again agreeing with Dorst's values. In general, almost two full months were required from the time of egglaying to the time the first nestling left the nest. However, the one early nest I was able to follow to completion in 1968 fledged two young only 22 days after hatching. The incubation period was the standard 20 days. Incubation and most of the care of the young of this nest were accomplished without interference from heavy rains.

Fledging was a relatively long process, usually occupying at least a week. One young was always more advanced than the other and left the nest one or two days earlier. The time spent out of the nest began with only a few minutes in the morning on the first day, during which flight was obviously weak. The fledglings often returned to the nest to roost at night long after the mother departed. This was especially true of female young: in 1970 six females (of nine followed) continued in their nests at least one month after fledging, while only one male young (of six followed) did. If the nest was built in satisfactorily sheltered areas, the young remained in the vicinity throughout the winter, the females in the nest, the males nearby.

Of nineteen nests followed to completion, eighteen began with 2 eggs and one began with 1 egg, giving a potential of 37 young. There were 15 egg or nestling mortalities, 8 of which were directly due to human interference (curious natives removing nest contents; females abandoning nests after disturbance). If these 8 are eliminated, there were 7 natural mortalities and 22 young fledged, making a natural breeding success of 68 percent. The seven mortalities were:

— one egg fell out of a nest.
— one mother deserted her one egg apparently because of persistent interference by another female.
— another mother deserted her two eggs after 20 days of incubation. I dissected the eggs: one appeared completely undeveloped and the other had a partly-formed embryo. The nest was under a metal roof and it seemed possible that fatally high temperatures may have occurred in this site.
— one young fell out of a nest.
— one young was found mummified in the nest at a very early stage of development; cause of death was unknown. The other nestling was healthy and fledged.
— one young disappeared from a nest during a week when I did not check that nest; the other young fledged successfully.

In addition to these nineteen nests, there were three inaccessible nests in which I could see and sex by plumage only one nestling or fledgling per nest with certainty. These fledglings could be included with those above to compute the percent of nests that fledged at least one young. Again, if human-caused mortalities are not considered, sixteen of eighteen nests (89 percent) were successful. The fledglings that were visible in the inaccessible nests could also be included in the following 2 x 2 contingency table constructed to determine if there were relatively more successes and fewer failures in nests built in the wild than in those built in or near human habitations:

	Successful to fledging	Failed to fledge	Total
Wild	19	6[a]	25
Human habitations	6	9[b]	15
Total	25	15	40

[a] three of the six were human caused.
[b] five of the nine were human caused.

By a Fisher's Exact Probability test, the percent nesting success was significantly higher in the wild than in human habitations ($p = 0.02$). Of the 25 successful fledglings (including the 3 visible fledglings in inaccessible nests) 13 were males, giving a secondary sex ratio of 1:1.

After the young fledge, the mothers disappear, leaving their nests to their young or to another opportunistic female nester, the latter of which may build upon the old nest. Building on top of old nests was a common occurrence (see Peña et al., 1964). I have no data to establish whether new females may displace fledglings of a previous female that maintain the nest as a roost site. Neither Dorst (1962) nor I were able to detect cases of second broods.

II. DISCUSSION: SEASONAL REPRODUCTION, NEST SITES, AND WINTER MORTALITY

Seasonal Reproduction

Most hummingbirds breed seasonally; in many of the species studied, the onset of the breeding season seems correlated with the blooming of nectar sources (Bent, 1940; Stiles, 1973). Although it is possible that *O. estella* does not breed in the dry season because of climatic stresses to its physiology and the necessity for nocturnal torpor (Carpenter, 1972; 1974), food availability for the young is probably also a major selective pressure for the restriction of breeding to the rainy season (cf. Stiles, 1973). *Cajophora* (Loasaceae) was always the main nectar source used by female *O. estella* in the breeding season in my study areas: the first blossoms appeared in September. About the same time many small dipterans became more available. The only abundant native plant used by the hummingbirds in the winter was *Chuquiraga spinosa,* which is not a rich nectar source and is not preferred by *O. estella* (p. 38). However, even in areas where nectar-rich *Eucalyptus* was blooming profusely in the winter, breeding did not occur in the winter months, even though in one area suitable nesting sites (known to be used in the summer) were within 30 m of a clump of nine trees. This is true likewise of *Calypte anna* in California where *Eucalyptus* also blooms during the bird's nonbreeding season (Stiles, 1973). Thus, food availability may not be a proximate cue for breeding. Because twice (both in 1968 and

1970) the first signs of breeding began before either an increase in food availability or the onset of rains, photoperiod may be the proximate cue for sexual resurgence as suggested for many other species of birds (Marshall, 1961). In southern Peru there is a two-hour difference between summer and winter daylengths. In Ecuador, where there is essentially no annual photoperiodic change, *O. chimborazo* breeds year-round (Smith, 1969). There also are no radical seasonal climatic or vegetational changes, so there should be no physical selection pressure for breeding seasonality. The necessity of a photoperiodic cue for breeding would explain why hummingbirds do not breed even when abundant artificial or introduced nectar supplies become available.

In light of the long breeding season, it is possible that females bring off more than one clutch per year. This is known to occur in *Calypte anna* (Legg and Pitelka, 1956), *Selasphorus sasin* (Pitelka, 1951), and *Archilochus alexandri* (Cogswell, 1949). It might seem energetically wasteful for the female to abandon her large nest after fledging her young. However, because the nest is in good condition at the end of the nestling period, there would be selection pressure for the mother to build a second nest elsewhere if the first nest can serve as a dependable, warm roost site for her fledged young, thereby increasing their chances of survival.

Nest Sites: Their Characteristics and Effects on Recruitment

Dorst (1962) reported that 12 percent of the nests he discovered were in vegetation other than *Puya raimondi*. He also found that 70 percent of the nests in rocks faced east, supposedly to take advantage of early morning warming by the sun. My data do not support either finding: I found no occupied nests in vegetation other than *Puya*, and the orientation of the nests was random with respect to the rising or setting sun. Smith (1969) also found orientation random in *O. chimborazo* and suggested that orientation simply depends upon the topographical situation of available nest sites. He found nests only in rocks and not in vegetation. Perhaps the discrepancy regarding nests in vegetation is because I dealt only with occupied nests, whereas Dorst included old nests in his data, thereby possibly including abaondoned, unsuitable nests never finished or used, or nests of *Colibri coruscans,* which are built in vegetation. Puna vegetation other than *Puya* would not offer the thermal advantages and security from weather and predators that rocks and *Puya* offer. In any case, it is apparent that most *O. estella* nests are built in unusually protected, inaccessible sites.

The unique nature of these sites for hummingbirds undoubtedly contributes to the extraordinarily high percentage of nesting success. Success values in other hummingbird species for which data are available are compiled in Table 5. Nest predation is thought to account for much nesting loss in other species, especially the tropical species. Yet not one loss in *O. estella* was attributable to nonhuman predators. Smith (1969) also believed nest predation to be unimportant in *O. chimborazo*. Peña et al. (1964) found evidence for lower success (47 percent) at the edge of the distribution of *O. estella estella* in Chile. Their estimate of nest loss was based on mummified young or unhatched eggs found in old nests, which implicates some nest mortality factor other than predation, perhaps weather. It would be interesting to obtain nesting success values for *Lamprolaima rhami* and *Panterpe insignis,* since these two montane species have been observed to nest under rocky overhangs at least occasionally (Wolf and Stiles, respectively — pers. comm. from Wolf).

TABLE 5
Nesting Success in Hummingbirds

Species	Number of nests in which eggs were laid	Number of nests fledging at least one young	% success of nests in which eggs were laid	Source
North American				
Calypte anna	68	30	44	Stiles, 1973
	16	8	50	Legg Pitelka, 1956
Calypte costae	29	12	41	Woods, 1927
Archilochus alexandri	47	15	32	Stiles, 1973
Selasphorus sasin	16	4	25	Legg Pitelka, 1956
Tropical				
Phaethornis longuemareus	9 (lumped data from two habitats)	3	33	Skutch, 1966
P. superciliosus	3	1	33	Skutch, 1966
Phaeochroa cuvierii	5	1	20	Skutch, 1966
Oreotrochilus estella	18	16	89	Present study

Dorst's (1962) data and my own both indicate that embryo development requires a fixed amount of time but that the rate of nestling development is variable, depending mainly on the weather. The total period from egglaying to fledging requires about 40 days in most hummingbirds (Lack, 1968), compared to about 60 days in *O. estella*. In a species vulnerable to nest predation or other causes of nest failure, short developmental periods should be selected for (Gadgil and Bossert, 1970). Because *O. estella* is relatively immune to nest predation and has a high rate of nesting success, it can afford the long developmental period. This same correlation between protected nest sites and long developmental periods occurs in some hole-nesting birds (Lack, 1968).

The gradual increase in numbers of individuals in one of my study areas during the first three months of the breeding season (Fig. 10) suggests that migration is minimal. Not all of the individuals that newly appeared in an area during those months were fledglings of known nests, however, so it is quite probable that some small fraction of the population makes at least local migrations, perhaps related to dispersal outward from their winter roosts. Other nectarivores are known or suspected to wander during the nonbreeding season: hummingbirds (Wagner, 1945; Stiles, 1973), African sugarbirds and sunbirds (Skead, 1963; 1967; others cited in Stiles, 1973), and Australian honeyeaters (Keast, 1968). In addition, bits of data suggest that some individuals may fly long distances (several km) between flower sources during the nonbreeding season (Ruschi, 1949, cited in Stiles, 1973; Carpenter and MacMillen 1973; 1975). This has been suggested for *O. estella* (Langner, 1973) on the basis that the nearest floral food sources to roosting localities that the author himself was able to find were up to 120 km distant. However, at one of my study sites I was able to account diurnally for the same number of individuals (five) found at night, and in the other study site I was able to account for two of the six found roosting in the area. The latter area was in topographically complex terrain and I felt certain that I had not located all patches of *Chuquiraga* available in the area. Therefore, because I was able to diurnally account for more than half of the individuals located at night and because *Chuquiraga* is patchy and occurs in complex terrain, I cannot feel confident in Langner's assertions.

My evidence, therefore, indicates that mortality may be extremely high during the winter, probably because of a combination of factors: low nocturnal temperatures, scarcity of food, and poor quality food. One additional bit of support for this is that the one *O. estella* individual that was weighed immediately after collecting in the winter was a 7 gm male, weighing the least of any male in my sample size of 13. This weight lies outside the 95 percent confidence interval for male body weights. Augmentation of populations during the breeding season is probably primarily by reproduction, then, not by immigration, although some small fraction of the populations may make local migrations seasonally.

The evidence for competition for nest sites suggests that the number of nest sites available may be one of the factors determining the number of breeding females, and therefore (given polygyny) the size of the population in general. This suggestion is supported by information presented in this study on territoriality, which indicates that food is not a limiting factor on the females nesting in gorges. This situation is reminiscent of pairs of hole-nesting birds, such as wood ducks (*Aix sponsa*), whose population sizes can be increased by simply supplying more nest sites (Jones and Leopold, 1967, and others). Pearson (1953) was the first to suggest that nest-site availability, determined by topography, could limit *O. estella* population size. Specifically, he thought that the number of caves might limit the population because he found nests only in caves and tunnels, one occupied nest to a cave or tunnel. Although *O. estella* does nest in other topographical situations as well, this does not negate the premise since nest-site requirements are specific and the number of topographical localities satisfying those requirements is small. Such a situation should select for nesting territoriality. In wood ducks, pairs are not territorial and several will attempt to nest in the same artificial nest box: nesting success is inversely proportional to the number of pairs occupying a nest box (Jones and Leopold, 1967). Nesting territoriality would eliminate such nesting interference. The relative importance of nest-site limitation in the summer and energy limitation in the winter on the population size of *O. estella* will be discussed after the section on energetics.

Although females nesting in human habitations exhibited relatively low nesting success, it is possible that these females would have bred in even more marginal habitat or would have been excluded from sites in the wild and thereby would not have bred at all. In effect, humans may be increasing the carrying capacity of the environment for *O. estella* by providing their buildings as nest sites. This has probably more important an effect on population size than has the introduction of winter-blooming *Eucalyptus,* which serves as an important food for the hummingbirds in the dry season (present study; cf. Stiles 1973).

The discovery that some young remain in the vicinity of the nest throughout the winter leads to speculation about gene flow. If the young often remain close to their place of birth, this would result in inbreeding. Gene flow between populations of *O. estella* in the Andes is likely to be slow anyway because of disjunctness of suitable habitat and therefore of *O. estella* populations and because of their sedentariness discussed above. Disjunctness of populations and inbreeding should favor high rates of taxonomic differentiation, which in fact seems to be the case in the actively speciating, white-bellied forms of *Oreotrochilus.*

Territorial Adaptations

Some aspects of territoriality in *O. estella* have been mentioned in previous sections. In this treatment I will consider "territory" to mean an area "within which the resident controls or restricts use of one or more environmental resources" (Wolf, 1969). I consider territorial "defense" to mean any active advertisement or aggression which plays a part in excluding other hummingbirds from the territory. The mere presence of the owner in the area seems to act as a kind of defense in hummingbirds, as other individuals are usually aware of that presence and tend to avoid it (Bent, 1940; Pitelka, 1942). In the present context "active defense" will mean actual chasing of an intruder by the owner.

I. BREEDING SEASON TERRITORIES

During the breeding season, which begins as early as late August and ends in April, the females defend territories but the males apparently do not. As described earlier, the females nest almost entirely in the gorges under rocky overhangs. In these gorges two different kinds of territoriality occur. One involves solitary females with combined nesting and feeding territories. The other involves females nesting semicolonially with separate feeding areas. I also observed two cases intermediate between the solitary and semicolonial habits.

1. Solitary females. I studied a total of 28 occupied nests, 19 in the wild and 9 in buildings or under their eaves. Two of the former and 2 of the latter were not categorized

as to the solitary or semicolonial habits of the females because of inadequate observations. In 12 of the 17 categorized nests that I studied in the wild, isolated rock outcroppings or ledges provided a single suitable nest site each. In addition, 3 of the 7 categorized nests built in human habitations were considered to be solitary because they were built under small archways (2 cases) or in a small, single-roomed hut (1 case) with adjacent feeding territories. In the wild, the rock outcropping of a solitary female was typically surrounded by the usual stretches of grassy slopes or of scrubby growth deep in the gorge (Plate 5). In such a topographical and vegetative situation, the females defended a combined nesting and feeding territory about 60 m on a side (see also Dorst, 1962) against both males and other females. They fed on the summer herbaceous flowers and flycaught on their territories. Defense was frequent, especially in the morning; it was characterized by perching on the highest outlook posts available on the territory, emitting a piercing trilling call when another hummingbird flew by, and chasing if a hummingbird entered and loitered on the territory. If they chased, they used the same trilling call used on the outlook posts, whereas the hummingbird that was chased was silent. Identical behavior occurred in the 3 females nesting in buildings; their feeding territories were outside the hut or archway and immediately adjacent to it. This is the same kind of female territory described by Dorst (1962), although he did not emphasize the feeding function of the territory. Since he presented a map of four adjacent territories and indicated nest sites, boundaries, and outlook posts, I will not present my similar data, which would be repetitive.

2. Semicolonial females. The second situation, semicolonialism, seems to occur rather rarely in this species. I saw it twice: once in a large barn, involving 2 females, and once in the wild, involving 4. In the latter case a stream gorge had a large, complex rock outcropping with many ledges and one cave, providing several nest sites in the same general area (Plate 6). The actual nest sites were invisible to the neighbors when they were on their nests. In this topographical situation, the females defended nesting territories having a radius as small as 1.5 m from the nest (i.e., 3 m between nearest neighbors) and they flew in divergent directions to arrive on separate feeding areas in the gorge within several hundred meters of the nesting area (Plate 6). A female would defend her nesting territory solely by chasing those neighbors or other hummingbirds who strayed within the range of visibility from her nest. There was no call advertisement from high perches in the area as in solitary females, although a female might trill while on the nest if a chase involving 2 other birds occurred nearby. Many chases occurred but usually happened when 2 females approached their nests from their feeding areas at the same time. The residents rarely fed within the general nesting area although there were abundant insects and one flowering cactus (*Opuntia*) used commonly by *O. estella* elsewhere.

The behavior of the 2 females in the barn, whose nests were 10 m apart, was identical to that of the 4 females in the wild. For example, in the barn the 2 females avoided each other by using different windows for flyways and arriving on separate feeding areas near their exits. Thus, these 6 semicolonial females behaved in a very different manner than the 15 solitary females.

Feeding areas are probably unlimited relative to the availability of nest sites since the sloping sides of the gorges that serve as feeding areas are expansive but the rock outcrops and ledges are occasional and separated by nonrocky terrain. Except for the feeding area of 1 of the 2 barn females, I never saw more than one hummingbird using the same feeding area, even in the instance where the separate feeding area and movements of the female occupant were both easily observed. Her feeding area was comparable in size to a large solitary nesting and feeding territory. My strong impression was that aggression on and competition for suitable feeding areas on the expansive gorge slopes was essentially nonexistent — a situation that contrasted strongly with the obvious aggression around nest sites.

3. Intermediate cases. Between these extremes of solitary and semicolonial territories were some intermediate cases of closely situated nesting territories that included only a very small feeding territory adjacent to each nest. I saw 2 such cases, involving a total of 3 females. In one case, 2 females were nesting under adjacent eaves of a large thatched hut. Their nests were invisible from each other, as was a patch of ground about 12 m x 5 m in front of each nest. The 2 females both advertised from low perches near their nests, avoiding entirely the peak of the roof that served them both and that was the highest potential outlook post. They flycaught from the ground or a low perch near their nest in the area that was invisible from the neighbor's territory. Because these feeding territories were small and lacked flowers, the females had to supplement their food intake. They each flew to separate presumed feeding areas: their flight paths were in the direction opposite to that which would take them past their neighbor's nest. After one of these females fledged her young and went elsewhere, the other changed her behavior and began advertising from high perches as in the case of solitary females.

The second intermediate case occurred in the wild in the same complex rock outcropping in which semicolonialism was observed. The face of the outcropping curved sharply at one end (shown to the right of Plate 6) so as to face in a direction differing by about 45° from that of the main face. This end of the outcrop provided one nest site with an adjacent feeding area: the nesting-feeding area was actively defended out to 15 m from the nest, an area out of view of the 4 neighbors nesting on the main face. Again, as in the other intermediate case, advertisement was from low perches, not from the top edge of the outcrop common to all five nests. Flycatching was the major feeding activity on the feeding territory, although the area provided a few blossoms. The female possessed a separate feeding area up the gorge from the rock outcrop. I never saw any of the 4 semicolonial females fly past this nest and up the gorge in the direction of this intermediate female's feeding area — in other words, they avoided this female and her areas.

The behavior of the 3 intermediate females, then, possessed some aspects of the behavior of solitary females (advertisement, albeit limited; feeding near the nest) and some aspects of the behavior of semicolonial females (modification of advertisement in response to nearness of neighbors; separate supplementary feeding areas).

II. THE MALE DURING THE BREEDING SEASON

I never detected a defended male territory during the breeding season. During the days, I occasionally saw solitary males feeding on the open hillsides that separate adjacent gorges. These hillsides are grassland possessing several species of Cactaceae used by *O. estella* and a fair abundance of small dipterans (Fig. 7). Occasionally, a male feeding or perching on an open hillside would become involved in aggression with another hummingbird — either a male or female *O. estella,* or a *Colibri coruscans.* If the male was the aggressor, he would emit the same trilling call used by territorial females; if he was chased he was silent. Although chases involving males did occur occasionally, no pattern of consistent territorial ownership appeared. Sometimes I would see a male "jetting" from one end of a gorge to the other without stopping, and once a male flew with a flickerlike swooping flight high in the air from one end to the other of a gorge with nesting females in it. More rarely, during the day I would see a male flying from one female territory to the next; on only one occasion did I see a male feeding on a female's territory. Intruding (?) males were usually immediately chased from the territory by the female owner. But on several separate occasions, involving different males and females, I saw the male "refuse" to be chased, remaining perched on the female's territory: the female perched near him after her abortive attempt at chase, upon which the male flew up, hovered less than a meter above her, and silently displayed the green gorgette and the white belly with its chestnut stripe, and even more striking to the human observer, held his tail fanned and immobile, showing the three pairs of white rectrices that contrast with the dark central and outer pairs. In all of these instances, the females involved already had eggs or young, and the male's display was followed by no apparent response by the females. Then the males flew off. Twice I saw males chasing females around their own nesting territories: territorial calls were conspicuously absent during these chases. In every major nesting area, such as a gorge or a group of abandoned thatched huts, one or two males roosted at night, the same individuals returning to the same roost site every night. Nocturnal censuses by flashlight showed that the total number of roosting birds always closely approximated the population size as estimated by diurnal observations. The sex ratio of "adults" (determined by attainment of full bill length as well as by adult colors in the males) was roughly one male to every two females.

III. WINTER FEEDING AREAS AND TERRITORIES

With the onset of winter, dramatic changes affect the ecology of *O. estella.* First, breeding ceases (Fig. 9). Second, population densities of *O. estella* decline from about four hummingbirds per hectare in favorable breeding habitat to one per hectare in favorable wintering habitat (Fig. 10). Third, growth and flowering of almost all herbs cease. Fourth, although the winter of 1970 was mild, usually nocturnal temperatures and relative humidities plummet (Table 1). Fifth, *O. estella* becomes much more selective of specific roost sites: they are not found outside caves as they are in the summer. Sixth, the incidence and duration of nocturnal torpor in the birds increase (Carpenter, 1974). Lastly, the peak of flowering occurs in the native "hummingbird flower," *Chuquiraga spinosa.* In areas with only native vegetation the use of *Chuquiraga* by *O. estella* makes up almost the entire time budget (data presented below) for feeding during the winter in both sexes; flycatching occurs only rarely and no other plants are available.

I have seen *Chuquiraga* stands in two situations: (1) widely dispersed plants covering large expanses of open hillside, and (2) closely spaced plants occurring in clumps in the bottoms of sheltered gorges. I watched two such hillsides and two such clumps of *Chuquiraga* during the winter. In all cases, it seemed that only one individual used the resource with no challenge from or interaction with another hummingbird. In the case of the clumps it was easy to keep the owner in view most of the time, but in the case of the hillsides it was impossible to watch the individual for more than a few minutes. I inferred that it was the same individual because (1) I never saw two individuals on the same hillside within my field of vision at the same time, and (2) the occupant of the hillside was always the same sex; i.e., I would never see first a male and then later a female on the same hillside, yet both sexes occupy hillsides and clumps in the winter. In all cases I made my observation in July and August in midwinter; thus I never witnessed the establishment of these winter feeding areas, only their use.

At one of my major study sites, a garden with winter-blooming, nectar-producing eucalypts had been introduced within a kilometer of a large *Chuquiraga* patch, and hummingbirds roosting midway between the two food sources spent no time at the *Chuquiraga*, whereas the garden was heavily used. *Calypte anna* also is known to commute up to 1 km to feed at *Eucalyptus* (Stiles, 1973). This suggests a preference for rich nectar-producing plants, or at least for *Eucalyptus*. Further evidence for this preference is that of 18 *O. estella* captured in the winter, 50 percent were found in two localities possessing eucalypts, whereas I had to search eight localities without eucalypts to find the other 9 birds. There was a third eucalypt locality where I located 4 more birds not captured. I had the definite impression that the hummingbirds tended to congregate in the eucalypt areas in the winter (however, only when good winter roost sites were available within 1 or 2 km).

Although no active territoriality seemed to occur in *Chuquiraga*, both sexes of *O. estella* are capable of establishing and maintaining highly defended, permanent winter territories. This occurs in areas where *Eucalyptus* trees have been introduced. I observed one stand consisting of eight trees in the vicinity of the hacienda building which I used as a base for my winter studies (Plate 7). Here at 4100 m the *Eucalyptus* bloomed only during the winter. Four territories had been established therein and were maintained from June to early August, when I left. Three of these were defended by females, the other by a male. All four individuals were accounted for in nocturnal censuses of the surroundings and leg bands proved them to be the same roosting individuals throughout the season. During the day, secondary sexual characteristics identified the male, and the individual-specific behavior of the three females indicated their identities (specific perch sites, flight paths, degree of dominance, proneness to call, etc.). Both sexes used the identical advertisement and defense tactics described above for a female with a combined nesting and feeding territory. It is important to emphasize that both sexes used the same complex trilling call of breeding females, and that calling was a major tactic used in both advertisement and chase. The male never resorted to obvious plumage displays such as those used by the breeding territorial males of North American hummingbirds. In fact, both sexes spent about 60 percent of the 11 daylight hours hidden among the foilage.

IV. DISCUSSION: COMPARATIVE ASPECTS OF TERRITORIALITY

Territorial systems in hummingbirds show some diversity. North temperate zone species are sexually dimorphic, the male being brighter and having a display and feeding territory during the breeding season. The female apparently mates on the male's territory and raises her young alone in an area not related to the location of his territory. She defends only a small nesting territory and apparently feeds opportunistically or on any flowers that happen to occur near the nest (Bent, 1940; Pitelka, 1942; Stiles, 1973). At the end of the breeding season, territories break down and the birds often migrate, adults and juveniles of both sexes establishing ephemeral, small territories as they go (Armitage, 1955). Upon arriving at their wintering grounds in Mexico or Central America, they are apparently subordinate to the resident species and do not establish permanent territories (Skutch, in Bent, 1940; Wolf, 1969; 1970). Ephermeral feeding territories are again established in the spring migration (Pitelka, 1951; Cody, 1968). The male Anna hummingbird, resident in California, switches from large breeding and feeding territories to small feeding-only territories at the end of the breeding season; nonbreeding females are not territorial and feed opportunistically or by poaching on male territories (Stiles, 1973).

In the tropics some variations on this theme of (1) male feeding and breeding territories, (2) female nesting-only territories, and (3) ephemerality of winter feeding territories were reported by Skutch (1951), Wolf (1969), and Stiles (1970, with Wolf). Several lowland species essentially do not defend territories during the breeding season when food is abundant and flycatching is the major feeding activity, but during the nonbreeding season both sexes defend shifting feeding territories in locally abundant nectar sources. This nonbreeding territoriality is similar in many respects to that of North American migrant hummingbirds (Stiles and Wolf, 1970). Another variant of the theme of male feeding and breeding territory occurs in *Phaethornis* spp. (Nicholson, 1931; Skutch, 1951; 1964; D. Snow, 1968; E. Snow, 1974) and *Hylocharis leucotis* (Skutch, in Bent, 1940: p. 453), the males of which defend small lekking territories and must feed elsewhere. During the breeding season, several of the females of one montane species (*Panterpe insignis*) defend small, permanent feeding territories within a large territory defended on all sides by a male who does not feed on the included females' territories (Wolf and Stiles, 1970). Both sexes of this species also defend permanent feeding territories in the nonbreeding season, but the inclusion of female territories within a larger male territory apparently no longer occurs (Wolf, 1969). All of these tropical species are sexually monomorphic in color.

All these variations considered, to my knowledge no territorial system yet has been discovered in a hummingbird species that possesses the degree of complexity and flexibility that occurs in *O. estella*, a sexually dimorphic species. The way that environmental constraints force complexity and flexibility upon this species are fairly obvious and are depicted in Figure 11. Some of the less obvious aspects of Figure 11 will be discussed below.

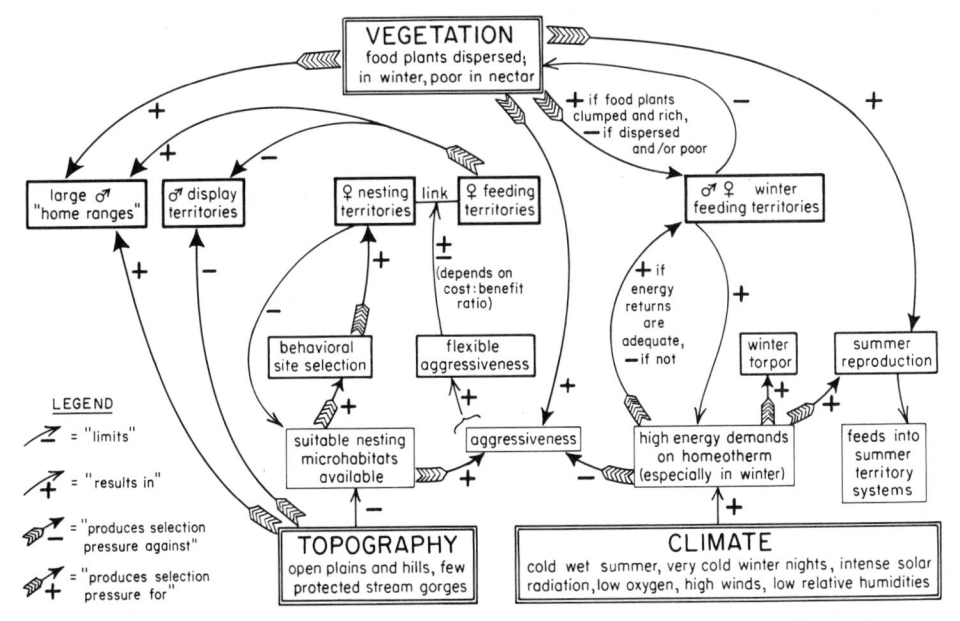

Fig. 11. Model of selection pressures affecting the territorial systems of *O. estella*. Boxes designating environmental selection pressures are outlined with double lines; kinds of territories affected by those pressures are outlined with heavy lines; intermediate effects of selection pressures are outlined with finer lines.

There seems to be a gradation in size of nesting territory among hummingbirds. Within *O. estella*, nesting-territory size depends on population pressure and topography although there are undoubtedly individual differences in tolerance of neighbors. This is reminiscent of the gradation of situations in male *Calypte anna* defending breeding territories (Stiles, 1973): a preferred territory is one with a self-sufficient food supply; the least preferred territories have little food and the males must feed in supplementary areas; intermediate cases exist, with some feeding on the territory and some off. Breeding-territory size in male *C. anna* thus is related to the dispersion of food supply, whereas in female *O. estella* territory size is related to the dispersion of nest sites relative to the food supply. In *O. estella* the preferred breeding territory is probably a solitary nest situation with a feeding territory adjacent.

Within the genus *Oreotrochilus* there are large differences in size of nesting territory in the two studied cases. In *O. chimborazo* as many as five females are known to nest in a 2 m radius (12 m^2) in a single cave (Smith, 1969). By contrast, the most crowded nesting area of *O. estella* had five occupied nests in 60 m^2 (Plate 6). Tunnels, caves, and small rooms in buildings are always occupied by only one nesting *O. estella* at a time (present study; Pearson, 1953). The case of *Oreotrochilus* suggests that the availability of nest sites relative to food availability may be the selection pressure determining species-specific differences in the size of nesting territory. That coloniality can result in severe nesting interference is obvious (present study; Jones and Leopold, 1967). Furthermore, coloniality can be disadvantageous because it costs more energy to have to fly from colony to feeding grounds. But as population pressure for limited nest sites becomes severe, nesting interference and energetic efficiency become less important as selection pressures, since the female is faced with the choice of breeding under crowded conditions or not breeding at all. Selection will favor persistence in establishing a nest site, tolerance of neighbors will increase, and territory size will decrease. This has reached an extreme (for hummingbirds) in *O. chimborazo*. It is quite possible that the few isolated volcanoes that comprise the range of *O. chimborazo* offer fewer nest sites suitable for the demands of this species (identical to those of *O. estella* – see Smith, 1969) than does the highly dissected and eroded mass of the Andes in southern Peru, and that the relatively seasonless and moderate páramo supports a larger potential breeding population than does the drier puna with its severe winter. The ratio of number of birds to number of nest sites therefore would be even greater in *O. chimborazo* than in *O. estella*, forcing more rapid evolution toward coloniality.

Eucalyptus, especially *E. globulus*, has become an important item in the diet of *Calypte anna* in California, particularly because it blooms during the season when other nectar producers are scarce. In fact Stiles (1973) believed that it has probably increased the carrying capacity of the environment for *C. anna*. The *Eucalyptus* in Peru also bloomed during the season of food shortage for *O. estella*. It probably has increased winter survival in the hummingbirds and thus the potential breeding population available in August. It probably has not affected the maximum potential population size, however, because of the limitation of available nest sites. One may speculate that in terms of evolutionary time, *Eucalyptus* might have an effect on population size by increasing the pressure for evolution of nesting coloniality, as discussed for *O. chimborazo* above.

The apparent lack of a defended male breeding territory in a typically color dimorphic hummingbird species has not been recorded previously. Dorst (1962) claimed to have seen male "display" territories in *O. estella* but did not describe them or the males' territorial behavior, if any, in detail. He did indicate that males tend to occur in more open habitat than do females, and he stated that a male's "territory" overlaps several female territories. These observations agree with mine, the only difference being that Dorst assigned the term "territory" (which in hummingbirds implies active defense) to the areas occasionally occupied by males and claimed that they are areas of breeding display. Smith (1969) reported the rarity of observing *O. chimborazo* males and observed in two cases that they seemed to occur in areas of their own separate from female nesting areas. He thought they "seemed" territorial in these areas but was unable to describe their territorial behavior or the characteristics of their territories. I believe that, in fact, *O. estella* males do not possess defended feeding and display territories. I also believe that the male displays I saw on female territories were the beginnings of courtship, initiated by the male. It appears that the males are opportunistic breeders and may have a kind of home range that includes a gorge of nesting females whose territories they occasionally visit in efforts to mate with any receptive females. This suggestion is reinforced by the facts that at night the same one or two males roost in the cliffs of the nesting areas, and that the adult sex ratio favors females, implying polygyny or promiscuity or both. Observations by Langner (1973) on *O. estella* in Bolivia seem to support this interpretation.

Since the females must nest in the gorges, and since it should be energetically favorable for them to feed as close to the nest as possible, then selection pressure is great for the females to use the slopes of the gorges for feeding areas. To accomplish this, the females had to evolve behavioral dominance to the males. Dorst (1962) also believed that males were subordinate to females. Thus, the females are able to fill up the gorges to the exclusion of the males. There is a supplementary manner in which selection may have brought about *O. estella's* unusual system. If a male home range indeed includes the territories of several females with whom he has probably mated, then it is also selectively advantageous for him not to compete intensely with those females, as is the case in *Panterpe insignis*. On the open hillsides the males feed on untapped, adequate but dispersed food supplies without overlapping the females' habitat during the day. The dispersion of the food supply on the hillsides would necessitate large size of the home range (Stiles and Wolf, 1970) and may explain why males are so rarely seen during the day. Evidence for habitat segregation of the sexes was given or cited for six of seven North American hummingbird species by Pitelka (1951), confirmed for *Calypte anna* by Stiles (1973), and indicated for *O. chimborazo* by Smith (1969). That females rather than males occupy the better foraging habitat is different from the North American hummingbird situation, but this is a consequence of the nest-site requirements and aggressive territoriality of the female *O. estella*.

The discussion above included comments on the selection pressures for breeding territoriality in female *O. estella*. What are the forces involved in the development of feeding territoriality? A territorial individual has greater control over its food resources than does a nonterritorial individual. Greater control means greater security because of greater resource availability and predictability. It also makes it possible for the individual to store energy for use in short-term emergencies. Feeding territoriality should be most obvious under conditions of food limitation and/or climatic stress or unpredictability.

Although food is probably not limiting to females during the breeding season, there is still some selection pressure for energetic efficiency. Although nesting is highly successful in this species, the nestling stage is still probably the most vulnerable of the whole life cycle because the young are helpless and subject to accidents. The young of more efficient females should spend less time in the nestling stage. As long as feeding territoriality increases her efficiency, then, a female should defend a feeding territory as close as possible to the nest.

In *O. estella,* feeding territoriality is most obvious, defense most violent, and control of resources most precise in the winter in rich food sources (*Eucalyptus*). Demands upon a hummingbird's energy reserves are likely to be the most severe in winter. Yet it is also the season when native food sources are sparse. Thus, although nest sites limit the breeding population in the summer, food limitation and mortality may be severe in the winter. Winter, then, determines the lows to which the population sizes fall and therefore the size of the breeding population at the beginning of the summer.

It seems that defensibility (Brown, 1964) and degree of richness of the food source (Stiles and Wolf, 1970; Wolf, 1970) can help explain why the demand and therefore competition for a *Chuquiraga* patch is low to nonexistent. Specifically, if *Chuquiraga* is widely dispersed and provides little energy, defensibility and richness are low and few hummingbirds should be attracted (see Heinrich and Raven, 1972); however, if it is clumped, defensibility is extremely high and richness is thereby increased slightly. Although attractiveness remains low compared to *Eucalyptus,* it should increase slightly as a result of the increased defensibility and lowered foraging costs. However, few interactions should be required for the establishment and maintenance of the clump as a feeding area because of its generally low attractiveness to others. For active defense to occur in *O. estella* in the winter, the food source must be both rich in nectar and concentrated in space, conditions which are never simultaneously satisfied by *Chuquiraga* but which are by *Eucalyptus.* Stiles and Wolf (1970) have shown that hummingbirds tend to cluster around richer food sources. Stiles (1973) offered some evidence that the time spent on defense by a territorial individual is directly related to the amount of food on the territory. The interplay between richness, dispersion, population pressure, and defensibility is presented in model form in the section below on energetics.

Equal defense of feeding territories by both sexes is atypical behavior in sexually dimorphic hummingbirds, but could be explained by the importance of the vocal role in territorial defense. In color monomorphic species in which the sexes defend feeding territories on an equal basis, vocalizations are the primary means of display (Skutch, in Bent, 1940: 443; Wolf, 1969; Stiles and Wolf, 1970). The apparent anomaly of a larger more brightly colored male having no territorial advantage over females may be explained because territorial defense (advertisement and/or chase) in this species is characterized by vocalizations rather than visual displays. Yet, the large size and bright color of the males should be selected for because his breeding success depends on his arriving on the territory of a receptive female and making an immediate, striking impression on her. This is contrary to the current thinking (Pitelka, 1942; Wolf, 1969) that bright color in hummingbirds is primarily for territorial defense and that mating occurs as a byproduct of territory occupation. However, display territories probably would be ineffective in *O. estella* because the male is excluded by the females to the open hillsides where females rarely occur in the breeding season, and where the grasses offer no prominent display perches from which to advertise in the "typical" hummingbird manner. Briefly, *O. estella* has color for courtship and trilling for territory.

It is noteworthy that the only hummingbird territorial system that approaches the structure and complexity of *O. estella's* is possessed by another tropical resident montane species, *Panterpe insignis,* referred to in the beginning of this discussion. Two critical environmental variables have resulted in the differences between *Panterpe's* and *O. estella's* territorial systems: the strict nest-site requirements of and limitation on the female *O. estella* and the dispersion of food supplies, both of which result in selection for exclusion of males to areas with very highly dispersed food resources. A male *Panterpe* is able to defend actively a territory large enough to provide for himself and one or more females simply because *Panterpe's* food resource is much more concentrated in space and therefore more defensible than are the extraordinarily dispersed food resources of male *O. estella* on the hillsides.

This section has shown that active defense of territories may or may not occur in *O. estella,* depending on the energetic situation of the birds and on pressure from neighbors attracted to the same area. The next section will present a model that predicts quantitatively under what circumstances defense will occur, and will quantify the energetic cost of territoriality to *O. estella.*

Energetics

I. METABOLISM AND TORPOR

Energy is a basic currency of ecological systems. This is why environmental physiologists have spent much time and effort determining metabolic rates of various organisms under various conditions. Yet all too rarely laboratory findings get translated back into the field in meaningful ecological terms. *O. estella* provides the opportunity to express adaptive traits studied in the field in terms of energy savings. To do this I had to make the usual metabolic determinations on resting and torpid *O. estella* in the laboratory. Section I will deal with metabolism in this species and comparisons with other hummingbirds, and Sections III and IV will use the laboratory measurements to assign quantitative adaptive values to the traits of *O. estella* that I have dealt with previously.

Materials and Methods

Toward the end of each of my three field periods in 1968 and 1970 I collected live hummingbirds from their roosts at night and kept them in cages like those described on p. 21. The birds were fed the sugar-protein-vitamin formula suggested by Lasiewski (1962). I experimented with various techniques for transporting the birds from the field to California — a 60-hr trip at best by foot, truck, train, and airplane. This species is too nervous to submit to a confining jacket as described by Lasiewski (1962) — the birds continue to struggle in spite of the confinement of their wings and eventually rub their shoulders bloody or twist within the jacket until strangled. The most successful transportation method employed carrying cases 22 x 22 x 60 cm, each of which was divided into two equal compartments equipped with a feeder and 22 cm perch. The walls were of soft tulle which prevented injury. Up to four birds per compartment could accommodate to these cramped quarters, and 100 percent survived the trip in this way with little or no damage to the plumage. Upon reaching California they were returned to spacious cages with no more than four birds to a cage. Feeders for each individual were placed in the corners and a shallow water pan was provided as a bath. The cages were kept in an insulated room on a 12-hr photoperiod and a temperature regime of 15°C during the day and 10°C during the night. Relative humidity varied from 45 percent (day) to 70 percent (night). The birds remained healthy in appearance for two to six months with this treatment, but eventually died. Ruschi (1961b) also was unable to maintain the species more than five months in his aviary. Data were not used from birds that appeared unhealthy. Almost all data came from 13 birds captured in July and August, 1970, that had acclimated to laboratory conditions for two to five months.

Oxygen consumption was measured over a 24-hr period, beginning and ending in early afternoon, with a Beckman G2 oxygen analyzer equipped with a Honeywell Electronik 15 recorder. Methods were similar to Lasiewski (1963). The high costs of hovering measured by Pearson (1950) were corrected for lower values found by other workers. See Hainsworth and Wolf (1972) for later comparisons between my results and Pearson's. My birds occupied 4.85 liter rectangular lucite chambers equipped with perch, small feeder containing a 20 percent sugar solution, thermistor for monitoring chamber temperature, and entry and exit ports for air. The feeder was placed so that the birds fed while perching. Three of these chambers were available and two birds and one control were run per day. The chambers were immersed in a controlled-temperature water bath circulated by a pump: temperatures within the chambers varied ± 1°C and will be referred to in this paper as T_a (ambient temperature). The water bath was maintained at a given temperature for several days until I had measured the oxygen consumption of an adequate number of birds at that temperature; then the bath temperature was changed for a series of measurements at the next T_a. Experiments were occasionally interrupted to take cloacal body temperatures with a thermistor connected to a Yellow Springs telethermometer model 43TD. No oxygen consumption data were used before four hours of equilibration in the enclosed chamber. The values used were the lowest values that were obtained by the bird during the 24-hr experiment and in general seemed to represent periods of perching without other activity. No more than one value was used for a given individual at each T_a at each of the three metabolic levels to be described. Air flow was maintained at 96 to 114 cc air/min. and was dried before and after leaving the respirometer chambers. Oxygen consumption values were corrected for standard temperature and pressure. The birds were weighed to the nearest 0.01 gm on a Mettler balance before and after each experiment.

Nocturnal body temperatures were recorded in separate experiments in a controlled-temperature room (± 1°C). Thermocouples made of 30 gauge copper-constantan wire were inserted 1.5 cm into the cloacas of roosting birds and secured by taping the wires to the base of the tail. Room and body temperatures were recorded on a Honeywell Electronik 16 from 1800 hr to 0600 hr, the dark period when the birds were immobile. "Body temperature" henceforth will be abbreviated T_b.

In this paper "torpor" means the state in which an animal that is capable of maintaining a high constant T_b by means of chemical heat production, allows its T_b to fall and remain at temperatures too low for coordinated muscular activity. Plate 8 shows the typical posture of a torpid hummingbird.

Observations on torpid birds were made in the field at night. Breathing rates were counted with a stopwatch and T_b was measured with a quick-responding Schultheis thermometer inserted 1.5 cm into the bird's cloaca. T_a in the roosts was measured either continuously with a Tempscribe (accuracy ± 1.0°F) or with a Taylor maximum-minimum thermometer (accuracy ± 1.0°F).

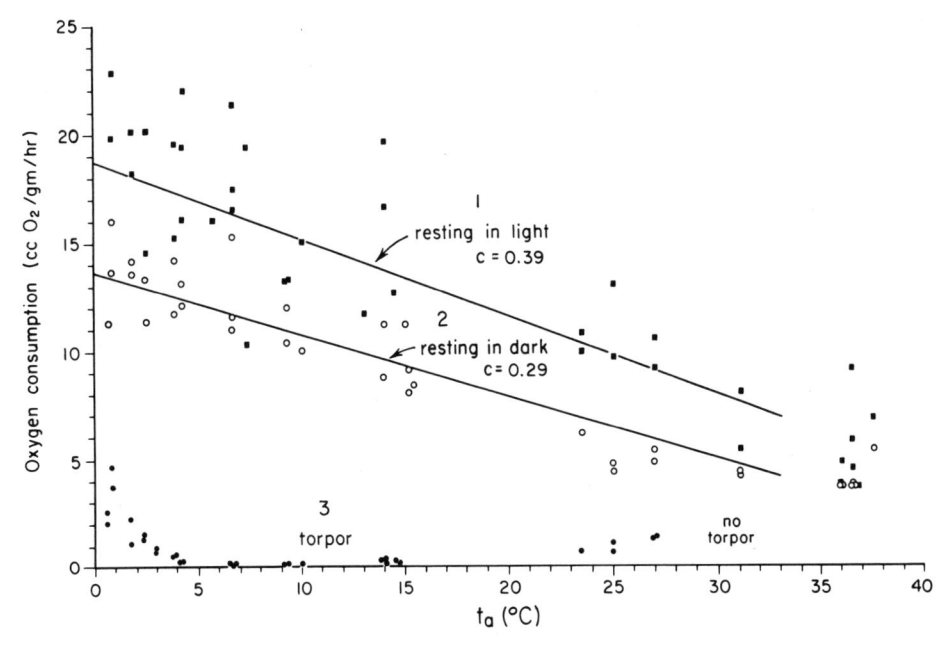

Fig. 12. Metabolism in *Oreotrochilus estella*. Oxygen consumptions at three metabolic levels are presented. The regression coefficient, r, for the metabolic level "resting in light" is 0.90 and for "resting in dark" is 0.94 (p < 0.01 in both cases). C, thermal conductance, is the absolute value of the slope of the line.

The equation for metabolism at level 1 is $\frac{cc\ O_2}{gm\ hr} = 18.77 - 0.39\ (T_a)$, with standard error of the estimate = 2.55.

The equation for metabolism at level 2 is $\frac{cc\ O_2}{gm\ hr} = 13.77 - 0.29\ (T_a)$, with standard error of the estimate = 1.35.

Results and Discussion

Figure 12 shows three levels of metabolism between $T_a = 0.75°$ and $31.0°C$: (1) the lowest oxygen consumption rates of birds resting during the day (T_b varied between 34° and 37.5°C; (2) the oxygen consumption rates of postabsorptive birds resting in the dark just before dawn (T_b varied between 33° and 35°C); and (3) the oxygen consumption of torpid birds (body temperatures to be described; torpor did not occur at $T_a = 31°C$). In addition, metabolic measurements were made on birds in the light and the dark at 36° to 37.5°C, during which T_b varied between 36.5° and 40.5°C.

Metabolic rates were relatively constant between 31° and 37°C T_a, corresponding to the zone of physical regulation or "thermal neutrality." Below 31°C the birds' thermal conductance should be minimal and regulation accomplished by chemical heat production; the slope of the line (Fig. 12) often has been considered to be a measure of thermal conductance, C. At metabolic level 1, C = 0.39 cc O_2/gm/hr/°C, and at level 2, C = 0.29 cc O_2/gm/hr/°C. T-test indicated no significant difference between these two values. The latter value is probably the more dependable since the birds are inactive and the data points show less scatter; this value for C is similar to the C = 0.30 found for the similar size *Eugenes fulgens* (Lasiewski and Lasiewski, 1967; Wolf and Hainsworth, 1972). C for an 8 gm bird should be 0.30 cc O_2/gm/hr/°C calculated according to the equation of Lasiewski et al. (1967), or 0.31 cc O_2/gm/hr/°C calculated according to the equation of Herreid and Kessel (1967).

Figure 12 shows that in torpid birds (metabolic level 3) oxygen consumption increased with T_a above 6.6°C, and that below 6.6° the birds chemically thermoregulated. Figure 13 shows the T_b of birds at metabolic level 1 compared with that of torpid birds. At T_a < 6.6°C, torpid T_b was maintained between 5° and 10°C, tending to increase slightly with decreasing T_a. Figure 14 indicates the exponential nature of torpid metabolic increase both above and below 6.6°C. The increase in oxygen consumption above 6.6° corresponds to a Q_{10} of 3.0 for the body temperature increase. The exponential increase in oxygen consumption below 6.6° is at least partially explained by the increase in T_b with decreasing T_a.

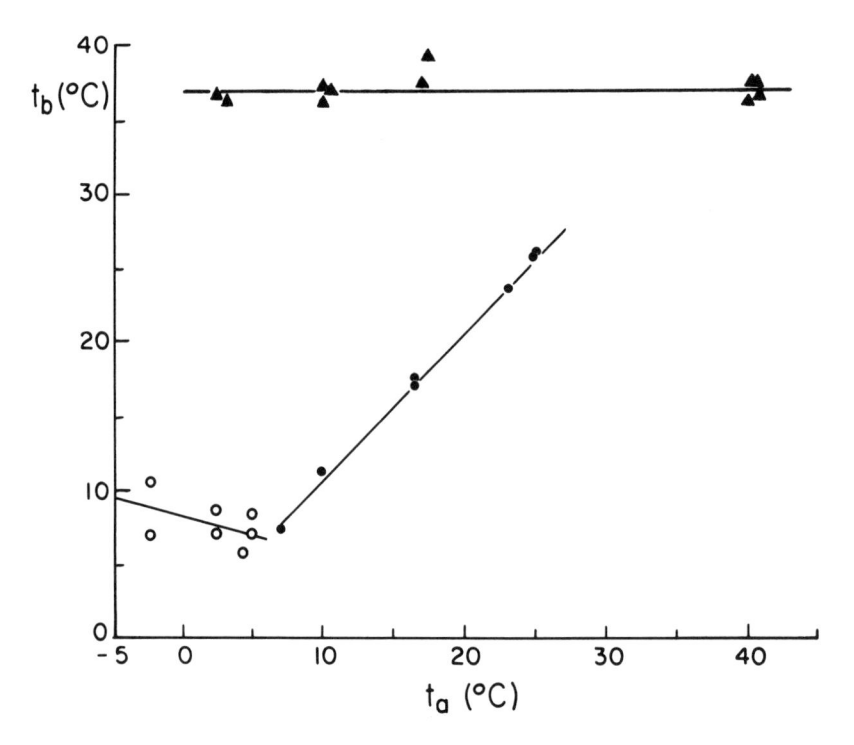

Fig. 13. Relation of T_b to T_a in homeothermy and in torpor. The slope of the line for homeothermy is not significantly different from 0. Slope = 0.99 for the line for torpor above 6.6°C (closed circles). The slope for the line for torpor below 6.6°C (open circles) is -0.22 but is not significantly different from 0.

Average minimum roost temperatures in the summer roosts were 6°C; in the winter roosts, 5°C. It is apparent from Figures 12 and 14 that in torpor the lowest rates of oxygen consumption occur between 6° and 7°C, temperatures similar to the average minimum nocturnal roost temperatures. Considerable energy savings occur between T_a values of 3° and 25°; below 3° regulation is expensive and at 1° oxygen consumption in torpor is equal to oxygen consumption in the zone of thermal neutrality during homeothermy. At 31°C and above, torpor does not occur. Only 6 of 72 minimum T_a values in the natural roosts of *O. estella* fell below 3°C. Langner's (1973) measurements of minima in the roosts of *O. estella* in Bolivia never fell below 5°C in the winter.

The T_a at which oxygen consumption is lowest (6.6°C) shares some characteristics with the zone of thermal neutrality. First, it is the T_a at which minimum energy is spent for that particular metabolic level: below it chemical thermoregulation of T_b occurs; above it T_b increases with T_a resulting in increased metabolic expenditure. Second, it is the T_a below which thermal conductance, C, must be minimal and above which C must be maximal. Because this T_a is important to the physiology of torpor it deserves a special term. I shall refer to it henceforth as the Temperature of Maximal Energy Savings, TMES. This temperature is actually both an ambient temperature and a body temperature: torpid T_b follows T_a closely as T_a decreases to the TMES; just below the TMES thermoregulation begins and T_b is maintained at about the TMES level, although T_b does tend to increase a few degrees if T_a continues to fall.

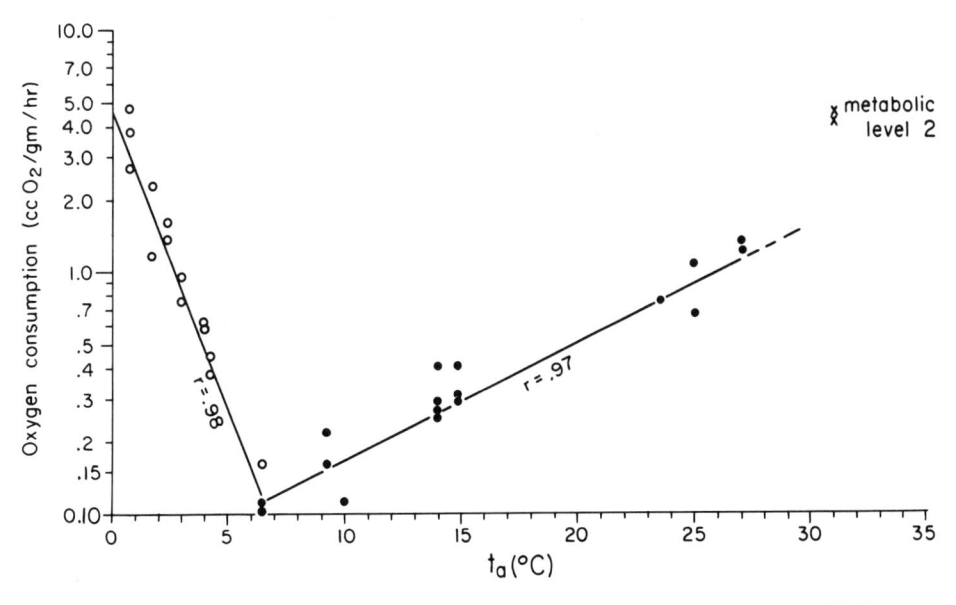

Fig. 14. Oxygen consumption in torpor. Semi-log plot giving regression coefficients for the two regressions. Oxygen consumption values for birds resting in the dark at 31°C are shown by x's.

Before performing the metabolic experiments in the laboratory, I had estimated that thermoregulation in torpor in the wild began between 5° and 7°C T_a. The minimum torpid T_b of a bird in the field was 5°C; the mean was 8°C. At 10°C T_a or higher the breathing of the birds was shallow but detectable. Between 7° and 10°C the birds entered long periods (up to 10 minutes) of apnoea that alternated with periods about 30 to 60 sec. long of deep regular breathing. Below 5° to 7°C, apnoea disappeared, deep regular breathing became continuous, and the lower the T_a, the faster the breathing rate. Thus, the observations on T_a, T_b, and breathing rates of birds in the wild predicted the laboratory results.

In both summer and winter, torpid birds in the field began arousal from torpor between 0230 and 0400 hr, or at least 1.5 hours before dawn. This was also true of healthy birds in the laboratory. From my field observations I formulated the following possible cues for arousal: (1) a sudden lowering of T_a that was often apparent on Tempscribe records one or two hours before dawn; or (2) depletion of food reserves. To test hypothesis (1) I placed 5 birds in one cage and 6 birds in another cage in separate temperature-controlled rooms (± 1°C) set at 8°C. At 0230 hr all 11 birds were torpid and showing periods of apnoea; I turned the thermostat of the room with 6 birds to 3°C. At 0330 hr the experimental room was 3° and all 6 birds were thermoregulating in torpor. No arousals occurred before 0400 hr and there was no significant difference between the time of onset of arousal of experimentals compared to that of the 5 controls. Thus, sudden lowering of T_a did not affect the time of onset of arousal.

To test the possible effect of depletion of food reserves I removed food at 1600 hr from an experimental group of 6 birds but allowed food consumption to continue until dark at 1800 hr in a control group of 2 birds. Again, there was no difference between the time of onset of arousal in the experimentals compared to that in the controls. Although the sample sizes were small the experiment indicated that, apparently, two hours of food deprivation before dark do not affect time of arousal, which suggests that arousal will occur at the same time of night regardless of the energy state of an otherwise healthy bird.

Thus, three potential cues have been eliminated as controlling mechanisms for timing arousal: the two external cues of light (see also French and Hodges, 1959; Calder and Booser, 1973) and of a sudden decrease in T_a, and the internal results of late afternoon food deprivation. If the arousal stimulus is internal and is timed by a "biological clock," that clock must be independent of temperature in the range of biologically important temperatures because arousal occurs at the same time of day regardless of body temperature or of the T_a regime during the night.

Discussion: Comparative and Adaptive Aspects of Torpor

Studies are accumulating which show that hummingbirds frequently become torpid at night in the laboratory (Pearson, 1950; 1954; Bartholomew et al., 1957; Lasiewski, 1963; 1964; Lasiewski and Lasiewski, 1967; Lasiewski et al., 1967; Tordoff, 1966; Wolf, 1967; Hainsworth and Wolf, 1970; Wolf and Hainsworth, 1972) and in the wild (Pearson, 1953; French and Hodges, 1959; Johnson, 1967). Studies of roosting hummingbirds are usually limited to accidental findings because most hummingbirds spend the night in vegetation and are difficult to locate. The records of torpor are inadequate for determining the incidence and significance of torpor to the wild hummingbird because laboratory studies could be dealing with an unnatural phenomenon that rarely occurs in the wild, and because the few records of torpor in the wild concerned individuals whose previous and subsequent histories remained unknown — the birds could have been moribund. Only a system in which hummingbirds could be located easily at night in the wild and studied *in situ* could answer questions concerning the actual significance of torpor to the birds. *O. estella* presented such an opportunity. My studies of the birds in the wild revealed that torpor commonly occurs on successive nights in healthy individuals and that torpor is therefore a real and an ecologically meaningful phenomenon in this species. The energetics of torpor will be discussed in Section IV.

The phenomenon of T_b regulation that occurs below the TMES of *O. estella* also is exhibited by the few other species that have been studied in this respect. Hainsworth and Wolf (1970) and Wolf and Hainsworth (1972) presented data for three tropical species: a large lowland species, a large highland species, and a small highland species. These data suggested the preliminary hypothesis that the temperature at which T_b is regulated (TMES) is correlated with the minimum average T_a characteristic of the typical environment of each species, rather than with body size. Data for two more species now can be added to support this hypothesis. In addition to the data for *O. estella,* data on T_b regulation in torpor are available for the desert-dwelling *Calypte costae.* Lasiewski (1963) presented a composite graph of torpor metabolism in four species of North American hummingbirds; although the data points are few, regulation in *C. costae* is apparent and was overlooked probably because its data points were lumped with those of the other species. Table 6 presents the data for *Oreotrochilus estella, Panterpe insignis, Eugenes fulgens, Eulampis jugularis,* and *Calypte costae.* In three of the species the minimum T_b of regulation corresponds almost exactly with the average minimum environmental temperature. In *P. insignis* and *E. fulgens,* two highland forest inhabitants, T_b of regulation is higher than minimum T_a but the climatic data came from a weather station, not from the actual roost sites themselves. I suspect that the minimal temperatures would prove to be much closer to 10°C if they could be measured in the roosts of the hummingbirds in dense vegetation.

It is apparent, then, that the T_b at which thermoregulation in torpor occurs, and therefore the TMES as well, are energetically critical and finely tuned to the environment within which the birds behaviorally regulate by roost selection.

TABLE 6
Comparison of Body Size, Regulated Body Temperature and Minimum Ambient Temperatures for Five Species of Hummingbirds

Species	Average Lab Weight (gm)	Minimum Regulated Body Temperature in Torpor (°C)	Average Minimum Environmental Temperature (°C)	
O. estella	8.1	5	5	(winter roosts)
P. insignis	5.0	10	5	(meterological report, Gov't. of Costa Rica)
E. fulgens	8.5	10	5	,,
E. jugularis	8.5	18	18	(Wolf, unpublished)
C. costae	3.0	20-22	19-24	(lab T_a, 9 months)

II. ENERGETICS MODEL FOR FEEDING TERRITORIALITY

As initially pointed out by Brown (1964) and as discussed in the previous chapter, several factors should determine whether feeding territoriality is economically feasible. If one or a combination of several factors become adequately favorable, the benefit of territorial defense should exceed the cost, a threshold should be crossed, and the individual should establish a territory. The following model is intended to incorporate all the major factors that determine the value of this threshold, and thus to allow energetic descriptions and predictions of the relative importance of each factor.

Th = Benefit − Cost

where Th = calories/time.

Benefit = f × n

where f = # flowers in territory

n = cals. of nectar secreted/(flower × time).

Cost = $M + ci + k_1 d_f + k_2 d_p$

where M = maintenance energy in cals. spent/time (energy spent while at rest or at flowers)

c = cals. spent/intruder

i = # intruders/time

k_1 = cals. spent in foraging flights/(meter × time)

d_f = mean distance between flowers (meters)

k_2 = cals. spent patrolling and displaying/(meter × time)

d_p = mean distance between advertisement perches (meters).

Thus,

$Th = (f \times n) - (M + ci + k_1 d_f + k_2 d_p)$.

When Th is less than zero, the bird cannot afford the cost of defense and must either cease defense or desert the area, assuming that it gets all of its energy requirements from the one area.

The energy spent chasing intruders is probably not linearly but exponentially related to the number of neighboring territorial owners: Stiles and Wolf (1970) showed that the number of chases per hour increased exponentially as the number of birds in the foraging tree increased, because the unoccupied volume in the tree decreased.

By mentally manipulating one or a combination of the parameters in the model, one can make several predictions. Given a situation where Th is just large enough to allow territoriality, the hummingbird should desert its territory if any of the benefit parameters decreases or if any of the cost parameters increases. Thus, territories should be deserted as flowering declines in an area, or upon the advent of blooming of poorer nectar species in exchange for the decline in blooming of richer nectar species even though absolute flower numbers might remain constant. Likewise, if maintenance energy should increase because of stressful climatic conditions, or if population pressure should increase because of recruitment or immigration, territoriality should disappear. For any set of conditions and parameters there should exist a threshold body size below which the species can be territorial but above which the species cannot be territorial because of the concomitant large value of M. The physiognomy of the terrain and dispersion of nectar plants will affect the value of Th under a given set of circumstances, because of the effect on d_f and d_p.

My observations on *O. estella* indicated the importance of the parameters i, d_f, and d_p. Recent work on Hawaiian honeycreepers (Carpenter and MacMillen, 1975) concentrated on the parameters of f, n, and M and showed that these do reach threshold values below or above which territoriality disappears. Studies of tropical hummingbirds support the prediction which the model makes with regard to body size. In a year when food was plentiful, a 10 gm species defended a larger territory than did two 5 gm species; in addition, the large species invariably hover fed thereby increasing M, whereas the smaller species sometimes perch fed (Stiles and Wolf, 1970). In this two-year study this same 10 gm species only defended territories in the year of more abundant flower availability, not in the year when flowers were sparser (the 5 gm species established territories both years). In another study (Wolf, 1969) *Panterpe insignis* males were shown not to defend their large territories very actively. This indicates that as d_f and d_p increase, there must be a compensatory decline in some other cost parameter, in this case k_2 and c.

This model is experimentally testable by manipulations of one or more parameters, such as gradual removal of flowers from a territory, artificial supplementation of n with sugar injections into flowers or addition of feeders, and/or reduction of i by removal of intruders. Rigorous tests of the model presently are being conducted (Ewald and Carpenter, in prep.) on *Calypte anna* using artificial feeders.

III. ENERGETICS OF LOCOMOTION

Other things being equal, a hummingbird that spends relatively more time in a day actively defending a territory and/or foraging will spend more energy per day than will a similar-size hummingbird that spends less time in these activities. This is because of the high cost of flight. In hummingbirds there are two kinds of flight, linear and hovering. Territorial defense usually involves the former and foraging the latter. This section will examine the costs of each of these kinds of flight.

Body Size and Linear Flight

The larger the bird the higher is the individual cost per km of linear flight. However, the cost does not increase linearly with the size of the bird. Instead, the proportion of increase declines with increasing body size: that is, the cost per km per kg of body weight declines (Tucker, 1970; Schmidt-Nielsen, 1972). If the proportion of the body weight comprised of fat as an energy store remains constant (at least over the small range of size observed in Andean hummingbirds), then larger birds having proportionally larger energy stores will be able to fly longer distances than will smaller birds. The greater weight-specific efficiency of larger birds should select for large size in species that must migrate, or otherwise fly long distances. The three hummingbird species in my study areas on the altiplano are all large. At least one of the two races of *Patagona gigas* is known to migrate and *Colibri coruscans* makes altitudinal migrations (Johnson, 1967). Some individuals of *O. estella* may make local migrations but a less speculative influence on size in this species is that since the food plants are highly dispersed compared to those in lowland habitats, relatively long foraging flights within a home range or territory are required. Thus, Andean high altitude selects for a large body size not only because of surface : volume considerations (present study) but also because of the dispersion of food sources and the tendency to migrate in high-altitude species.

I calculated the weight-specific costs of flight in these three Andean species and in *Calypte anna* for comparison, according to the empirically derived equation of Tucker (1970):

$$\frac{kcal}{kg\ km} = 1.25\ W^{-0.227} \qquad \text{(equation 1)}$$

where W = body weight and the standard error of the estimate = 0.186 log $\frac{kcal}{kg\ km}$.

TABLE 7
Calculated Cost of Linear Flight for Four Hummingbirds

Species	Weight	Cost of flight ± 2 standard errors of the estimate	95% confidence interval
Calypte anna	4 gm	4.38 ± 0.24 $\frac{Kcal}{Kg\ Km}$	4.14 - 4.62 $\frac{Kcal}{Kg\ Km}$
O. estella and *Colibri coruscans*	8	3.74 ± 0.21	3.53 - 3.95
Patagona gigas	20	3.04 ± 0.18	2.86 - 3.22

The one value Tucker (1970) calculated for hummingbirds assumed a flight speed of 49 km/hr and fits the regression well. Table 7 compares weight-specific costs of linear flight in the four species. The 95 percent confidence intervals of cost for each weight category do not overlap: *C. anna* spends 17 percent more per gram and *Patagona* spends 19 percent less than does *O. estella*, and these differences are significant at the 0.05 level in spite of the large standard error of the equation caused partly by different morphologies. The minor differences in body size in male and female *O. estella* will not result in significantly different costs of flight analyzed in this way. However, because males are significantly larger than females yet the wing length to body weight ratio is the same in male and female *O. estella* (9.35 and 9.36, respectively), the weight-specific cost of flight is significantly less in males than in females. By way of a specific though hypothetical example, if both sexes of *O. estella* carry 10 percent of their body weight in the form of fat metabolizable for flight energy, males would carry 0.88 gm and females 0.80 gm. From equation 1, one kilometer of linear flight would place a total cost of 32 cals on the male and 30 cals on the female. Assuming 1.0 gm fat yields 9.5 kcal of energy, the entire fat store of the male would carry him 261 km while that of the female would last 253 km. Theoretically, this difference, although small, would be statistically significant since it is weight related and the differences in the weights of the sexes were significant. Higher weight-specific efficiency of linear flight may be the prime selection pressure for large body size in the males, since their food supplies in the summer are more highly dispersed than those of females and they probably fly longer distances in search of food and of mates than do the females.

Wing Disc Loading and Hovering Flight

Pennycuick (1969) showed that the power output required for hovering flight can be calculated according to the equation:

$$P_{hov} = \frac{W^{3/2}}{(2\rho A_{WD})^{1/2}} + 0.887 \frac{W^{3/2} A^{1/4}}{\rho^{1/2} (A_{WD})^{3/4}} \quad \text{(equation 2)}$$

where P_{hov} = total power required in watts
W = body weight
ρ = air density
A_{WD} = wing disc area, given by $\pi\left(\frac{\text{wing span}}{2}\right)^2$
$A = 15.5 \frac{W^{2/3}}{400}$.

Epting and Casey (1973) showed that, among the 40 hummingbird species for which they made calculations, the differences in wing disc loading were enough to result in significant differences in P_{hov} between different species. Thus, a species can reduce significantly the cost of hovering (or of linear flight also) by evolving longer wings. One environmental characteristic of the high-altitude habitat should select for longer wings in resident hummingbirds — the lowered air density (ρ). I mentioned earlier that at 4000 m cost of hovering increases by some significant amount over the cost at sea level. Yet there is no compensatory increase in wing length relative to body weight in *O. estella* (Fig. 3). One could argue then that an alternative strategy for *O. estella* would be to relinquish hovering ability and forage entirely by perch feeding. This could easily happen while selection operated to increase body weight if the wing length did not increase proportionately. Yet this also has not happened in *O. estella*. Instead, this species has maintained an average wing disc loading and therefore the ability to hover when energy supplies are adequately available. These supplies should be made even more available by hovering (e.g., nectar from *Bomarea*). *O. estella*'s behavioral plasticity compensates for the relatively high cost of hovering at high altitude by increasing the proportion of perch feeding when energy is limiting (Fig. 5). It is noteworthy that the one species of hummingbird flower whose structure forces the birds to hover (*Bomarea dulcis*, Plate 1) blooms during the season when energy is not limiting, and that the one native plant blooming during the energy-limited season provides a convenient perch for the hummingbirds (Fig. 6). The energetics of these plants and of *O. estella* are intertwined with one another and with the climatic regime of the physical environment.

I calculated, using equation 2, that the power output required for hovering for *O. estella* at 4000 m is 16.1 cals/gm hr. Hainsworth and Wolf (1972) determined that the efficiency of converting metabolic energy into the power output of hovering in humming-birds is about 5.5 percent. This means that the metabolic rate while hovering will be about 18 times the power output required, or 290 cals/gm hr for *O. estella* at 4000 m.

IV. ENERGY BUDGET OF *O. ESTELLA*

Information from behavioral, reproductive, and territorial adaptations, carefully timed observations of the behavior of several individuals for several entire days, and nocturnal observations on roosting and torpor enabled estimation of time and energy expenses for 24-hr periods. The data are derived from breeding females and from both sexes in the winter experiencing different energetic and territorial regimes. The results are presented in Tables 8 and 9A, and the methods of calculation described in Table 9B. It should be emphasized that the results are based on a 24-hr period of activity so that, to determine the relative contribution that a single kind of activity makes to the daytime budget of the animals, one must allow for energy expenditure during nocturnal roosting.

TABLE 8

Time Allotments for Activities on a 24-Hour Basis
(Top values = hours, bottom values = % of 24-hour period)

	Diurnal perching resting incubating brooding	Diurnal perching perch feeding	Flight hover feeding linear flying	Flycatching	Territory	Nocturnal Roosting
1. a. Incubating or Brooding ♀ (N = 2)	7 hr. 29.2%	0.4 hr 1.7%	1.0 hr 4%	3.6 hr 15.1%	1.0 hr 4%	11 hr. 46%
1. b. ♀ feeding advanced young (N = 2)	0.8 hr. 3.2%	1.5 hr 6.2%	2.9 hr. 12%	6.9 hr. 28.6%	1.0 hr. 4%	11 hr. 46%
2. a. Winter ♂ in *Chuquiraga* (N = 1)	6.3 hr. 26.3%	4.0 hr. 16.8%	0.5 hr. 2.1%	0.2 hr. 0.8%	0 hr. 0%	13.0 hr. 54%
2. b. Winter ♂ and ♀ in *Eucalyptus* (N = 2)	5.0 hr. 21.1%	2.2 hr. 9.2%	0.8 hr. 3.3%	1.5 hr. 6.2%	1.5 hr. 6.2%	13.0 hr. 54%

TABLE 9A

Energy Allotments for Activities on a 24-Hour Basis in Kcals

	Diurnal perching		Flight	Flycatching	Territory	Nocturnal roosting			Totals (Kcal/Day)		
	resting incubating, brooding	perch feeding				with torpor at roost T_a / outside T_a	without torpor at roost T_a	outside T_a	with torpor at roost T_a / outside T_a	without torpor at roost T_a	outside T_a
1. a. Incubating or Brooding ♀ (N=2)	3.9	0.2	1.7	6.1	1.7	0	4.8	5.7	—	18.4*	19.3
1. b. ♀ feeding advanced young (N=2)	0.4	0.9	4.9	11.7	1.7	0	4.8	5.7	—	24.4*	25.3
2. a. Winter ♂ in *Chuquiraga* (N=1)	3.5	2.4	0.8	0.3	0	1.5 / 5.9	6.2	8.3	8.5* / 12.9	13.2	15.8
2. b. Winter ♂ and ♀ in *Eucalyptus* (N=1 ♂, 1 ♀)	3	1.3	1.6	2.5	2.5	1.5 / 5.9	6.2	8.3	12.4* / 16.8	17.1	19.7

*energy expenditure of the bird under the usual conditions.

TABLE 9B

Assumptions and Methods of Calculation in Table 9A

	Diurnal perching		Flight	Flycatching	Territory	Nocturnal roosting	
	resting, incubating, brooding	perch feeding				with torpor	without torpor
1. a., b. Breeding Season	Metabolism calculated hourly based on time-course of T_a in Fig. 8 and on: resting metabolic rate at normal T_b (level 1, Fig. 12).	2× resting metabolic rate (level 1 in Fig. 12). (Hainsworth Wolf, 1972).	All 3 flight categories are assumed to consist solely of linear flight as only 8% of 1 category, "Flight," is hovering flight (Fig. 5). Metabolism assumed = 212 $\frac{cal}{gm\,hr}$ (Lasiewski, 1963, and Tucker, 1970)			Torpor does not normally occur in breeding ♀♀.	Metabolism calculated hourly based on time-course of T_a in Fig. 8 and on metabolic rate resting in dark (level 2, Fig. 12).
2. a., b. Winter	Metabolism calculated hourly based on time-course of T_a from Tempscribe data and on metabolic rate resting: at $T_b =$ 34°C (level 2, Fig. 12).	at normal T_b (level 1, Fig. 12).	In *Eucalyptus* only, 60% of the "Flight" category is assumed to consist of hovering, 40% of linear flight (Fig. 5). Metabolism of hovering = 290 $\frac{cals}{gm\,hr}$ at 4000 m elevation (see section III). In *Chuquiraga* all flight is linear. The remaining 2 flight categories are assumed to consist solely of linear flight.			Metabolism calculated assuming 1.5 hr to enter torpor, 9 hr in torpor, 0.5 hr to arouse from torpor, and 2 hr resting in dark just before dawn.* Time-course of T_a based on Tempscribe data w/ minimum T_a outside roost = -2°C.	Metabolism calculated based on 13 hr at metabolic level 2 (Fig. 12) and on Tempscribe time-course of T_a.

*Cost of entry and arousal were estimated from appropriate metabolism experiments in the laboratory.

Several points should be made. First, breeding females have the highest energy expenditure of any individuals evaluated in spite of energetic savings from their heavily insulated nests (Calder, 1973) and warm nest sites. Furthermore, the female's expense increases when her young mature and demand more food. This increase is caused mainly by increased flights to and from foraging areas and increased flycatching. Second, hummingbirds overwintering in *Chuquiraga* patches have the lowest energy expenditure, mainly because they do not actively defend territories and because they perch feed and apparently obtain their protein from the plants, thereby making expensive flycatching unnecessary. Third, winter torpor conserves a great deal of energy — 36 percent in the *Chuquiraga* male roosting in a cave, and that value is based on the entire 24-hr energy budget! Similarly, the ability to roost in caves rather than on vegetation saves 34 percent in winter.

Previous discussions revealed other aspects of the behavior of *O. estella* which reduced the daily cost of living, especially in the winter, and of reproduction. Examples were: the restriction of breeding to the season of warmer nights, the female's defense of a feeding territory adjacent to her nesting territory, the avoidance of conflict situations when territories are crowded, and the flexibility of winter territorial aggression depending on the energetic rewards of the food supply. Another energy-saving device employed mostly in the winter is the adoption of long periods of total immobility during the middle of the day. For the major part of six hours, from 0900 or 1000 hr to 1500 or 1600 hr, the birds perched among shrubby vegetation, on shaded rock ledges, or in *Eucalyptus* foliage, and literally did not move for 45 minutes to an hour; even the usual alert motions that hummingbirds make with their heads during perching were absent. Large insects flying within centimeters of their heads elicited no response. Then the hummingbird would stretch its wings and fly to feed for about 10 or 15 minutes, at the end of which time it would return to the same shaded spot for another trancelike bout of up to an hour. Occasionally, perch sites were changed in order to maintain a position in the shade. Shade temperatures were about 15°C in the winter in midday. It is possible that the birds lower their body temperatures during these "trances." Lowered body temperatures, even by only a couple of degrees, could result in substantial saving of energy.

Three previous studies dealt with time and energy budgets of hummingbirds. Pearson (1954) and Stiles (1971) worked with *Calypte anna* and Wolf and Hainsworth (1971) worked with *Eulampis jugularis*. It is striking that *O. estella* tends to spend less time perching (about 50 percent of the daylight hours) and more time feeding (about 40 percent) in both seasons than do *C. anna* or *Eulampis* (about 80 percent and 10 percent respectively). This is presumably because the food supply of *O. estella* is more dispersed and/or poorer in quality and T_a may be lower. Also, the total energy requirements of *O. estella* are greater than those of *C. anna* (1.3 - 4 times greater), partly because they are twice as large as *C. anna*, but also, again, because of the dispersion of their food and the low temperatures of their habitat. However, the increased time spent feeding by *O. estella* is partly compensated for, especially in the winter, by the decreased energy required for perch feeding rather than hovering.

Table 10 compares the time and energy budgets of *O. estella* during the most energy limited season (winter) with those of a hypothetical "typical" hummingbird of similar size transplanted suddenly to the altiplano. This obviously is a purely hypothetical comparison and requires several simplistic assumptions, but nevertheless is an aid in visualizing the relative values of the most dramatic adaptations of *O. estella*. The assumptions are that this hypothetical hummingbird:

TABLE 10

Comparison of Energy Expenditures of *O. estella* and a Hypothetical Hummingbird, both in *Chuquiraga* in the Winter

	Diurnal perching		Flight		Nocturnal roosting		Totals (Kcal/Day)
	resting	perch feeding	linear and flycatching	hover feeding	torpid in caves	nontorpid in trees	
Winter ♂ in *Chuquiraga**							
time	6.3 hr	4.0 hr	0.7 hr	—	13 hr	—	
energy	3.5 Kcal	2.4 Kcal	1.1 Kcal	—	1.5 Kcal	—	8.5
Hypothetical "typical" hummingbird							
time	6.3 hr	—	0.7 hr	4.0 hr	—	13 hr	
energy	3.5 Kcal	—	1.1 Kcal	9.3 Kcal	—	8.3 Kcal	22.2

*2a from Table 9A.

1. has similar metabolic expenditures for each category of activity as does *O. estella,*
2. must spend an equal amount of time obtaining food from this environment as does *O. estella,*
3. is unable to perch feed and must hover,
4. roosts in the usual hummingbird manner in vegetation,
5. also does not defend a winter territory in the wild, and
6. is unable to maintain torpor at the low T_a characteristic of such roost sites in the winter and must spend the night homeothermically (assume $T_a = -2°C$).

Table 10 shows that this hypothetical hummingbird, not adapted for life at high altitude, would spend 2.6 times more energy than *O. estella.* By working with the information from both Tables 9A and 10, the savings can be broken down into categories (Table 11).

TABLE 11
Relative Values of Three Adaptive Traits of *O. estella*

Hypothetical situation	Trait concerned	Resultant 24-hr energy budget (Kcal/day) for hypothetical situation	Proportional increase in energy budget over that of *O. estella*
1. A bird that must hover feed	perch feeding	15.4	1.8
2. A bird that must roost in trees but could maintain torpor at low T_a	cave roosting	12.9	1.5
3. A bird that could not maintain torpor but could roost in caves	special torpor physiology (including low TMES)	13.2	1.6
4. A bird that could neither maintain torpor nor roost in caves	combined 2 and 3	15.3	1.8
5. A bird that possessed none of the three traits (see Table 10)	combined 1, 2, and 3	22.2	2.6

If the hypothetical bird could perch feed, it would spend only 1.8 times more energy than *O. estella.* If it could roost in caves but not perch feed, it would spend 1.5 times more than *O. estella.* If it possessed the same torpor physiology as *O. estella* but could not perch feed or roost in caves, it would spend 1.6 times more than *O. estella.* Thus, the three major adaptations in *O. estella,* perch feeding, cave roosting, and low TMES, are all of approximately equal value in reducing the cost of living at high elevation.

Another striking comparison seen in Table 9A is the seasonal change in energy expenditure in *O. estella,* lacking in *C. anna,* which from preliminary work (Pearson, 1954; Stiles, 1971) seems to spend about the same amount of energy (6 kcal/day) regardless of season or breeding condition. However, Pearson and Stiles worked with males whereas I worked with females in the breeding season and with both sexes in the winter. Perhaps female *C. anna* would show a similar increase in cost during the breeding season as did my female *O. estella.*

Lastly, territoriality seems to cost *O. estella* a constant amount (about 2 kcal/day) regardless of the season, except in the *Chuquiraga* situation. This was not true for *C. anna* males, which spend about 1 kcal/day defending breeding territories but only 0.2 kcal/day defending nonbreeding feeding territories (Stiles, 1971).

Although *O. estella* generally spends more total energy in its environment than do *C. anna* and *Eulampis* in theirs, its adaptations maintain those expenses at almost one-third of what they would be in a typical hummingbird in the Andes. The three adaptations that reduce its energetic costs the most are perch feeding, cave roosting, and low TMES.

V. INTERSPECIFIC INTERACTIONS

Interspecific competition and avoidance of predators other than nest predators can be energetically expensive. How costly are these to hummingbirds in general and to *O. estella* in particular? Adult hummingbirds are not noted to be a common prey item (Skutch, 1973), and evidence concerning the importance of predators to hummingbirds is indirect. Several species studied in Costa Rica showed apparent fear responses to approaches of large flycatchers and a turkey vulture (Stiles and Wolf, 1970). The potential diurnal and nocturnal predators that could affect *O. estella* were listed previously. Of these, I have seen *O. estella* mobbing *Falco sparverius* and *Felis colocolo*. The cryptic dorsal coloration of the various *Oreotrochilus* species and the possible antipredator function of the skin odor implicate predators as at least a mild selective pressure. However, neither Smith (1969), Dorst (1962), nor I have ever seen an example of predation on either adults or nests. The roost sites make this species almost invulnerable to nocturnal predation, and the striking lack of alertness during winter midday trances suggests that diurnal predation is rare. The birds probably rely mainly on their small size and cryptic coloration to avoid diurnal predation, thus spending little energy in predator-avoidance behavior.

In most hummingbird species great amounts of time and energy are often spent in interspecific strife (Bent, 1940; Pitelka, 1951; Stiles and Wolf, 1970; Wolf, 1970). This suggests that competition may be severe among sympatric species, not a surprising hypothesis since the food habits and behavioral characteristics of hummingbirds are similar and many species are thought to be food limited (Pitelka, 1942; Legg and Pitelka, 1956; Wolf, 1969; Stiles and Wolf, 1970; Wolf and Stiles, 1970; Stiles, 1973). Several of the above references give evidence that niche overlap is reduced among different species by habitat segregation. In southern Peru *O. estella* experiences few interspecific competitive interactions. *Patagona gigas* is rarely seen on the altiplano, although it occurred sympatrically with *O. estella* in my northern Chile study sites in the "spring." On one occasion an *O. estella* was feeding from a *Cajophora* plant when two *P. gigas* appeared and began to feed on the same plant. The *O. estella* perched a few meters away, waited until the *P. gigas* departed, and then resumed feeding. *P. gigas* is 2.5 times larger than *O. estella* and seemed dominant to it. Dominance hierarchies among species of hummingbirds are sometimes based on size, the larger birds being dominant (Wolf, 1970). Interactions with *Patagona* are not energetically costly to *O. estella*.

Colibri coruscans occurred in low numbers on the altiplano in the breeding season, which is the season when *O. estella* populations are probably not food limited. In my studies, *Colibri* only frequented areas with *Polylepis* or *Eucalyptus* trees. Five out of fifteen study sites had trees and of these, three sites supported some *C. coruscans*. Densities were low, two to four birds per site. A few cases of interspecific chases with *O.*

estella occurred, and *C. coruscans* always initiated the chases. Once a male *O. estella* was chased out of my sight; several cases of aggression on female *O. estella* occurred, but the females simply took refuge in caves or other dark places where *C. coruscans* refused to go. This is reminiscent of Brown's (1971) study on chipmunks in which the behaviorally subordinate species was also more generalized in habits and could escape aggression from the ground-specialized dominant by retreating to the branches of bushes. This kind of dominant specialist and subordinate generalist relationship also occurs in other hummingbirds (Colwell, 1973) and in honeycreepers (MacMillen and Carpenter, in prep.). See Morse (1974) for a theoretical treatment showing the relation between narrowness of niche and behavioral dominance. Because the numbers of *C. coruscans* are low, and because *O. estella* is able to retreat to places inaccessible to the dominant, it appears that niche overlap and competition with *C. coruscans* is minimal during the breeding season. In the winter when food becomes limiting, *C. coruscans* migrates to lower altitudes. At my 1970 winter study sites on the east flank of the Cordillera Oriental, *O. estella* was collected at 4000 m but was not seen lower, while the highest *C. coruscans* was collected at 3400 m. In 1968, I collected a *C. coruscans* at 3100 m on the west flank of the Cordillera Occidental in August (winter); the lowest *O. estella* has been seen at that same elevation in September (Pearson, pers. comm.).

In summary, little energy is spent by *O. estella* in predation avoidance in spite of the occurrence of fair numbers of potential predators on the altiplano. Likewise, little energy is spent on competitive strife in my study areas because of low numbers of other hummingbirds and because *O. estella* is a generalist and behaviorally subordinate to other hummingbird species.

Concluding Discussion

I. *O. ESTELLA* IN THE HIGH ANDES – A SYNTHESIS

The Selection Regime in Southern Peru

In the Introduction, I pointed out the general characteristics of the high-elevation habitat of *O. estella* in southern Peru and suggested that these characteristics might act as unusual selection pressures on members of the family Trochilidae. During the course of the study, a much more detailed and refined picture of the selective regime emerged.

As expected, the vegetation structure has been of major importance to *O. estella*. The physiognomy of the plant community has forced ground-dwelling habits on the birds, and the necessary adaptations for these habits have had wide ramifications on the birds' foraging techniques and energetics. The birds had to perch on the ground for flycatching and territorial posts, and the large feet evolved for this (and for other reasons) enabled them to perch feed at most flowers. This was a major energy-saving development, stemming partly from the physical structure of the environment. But in addition, it also became clear during the study that the blooming seasons of the different hummingbird plants and the structure and nectar reward of their flowers played important roles in the evolution of a flexible foraging strategy (both flycatching and flower feeding) which changes with season, with habitat, and with types of blossom used. Furthermore, the dispersion of food plants was found to be an important selection pressure, and to differ in the environments of the males and the females, with dispersion being greater in that of the male. This discovery then led to speculation regarding the importance of large body size in flight efficiency, and helped explain the size dimorphism in the sexes, since large body size confers greater weight-specific efficiency in linear flight.

Also as expected, climate has been crucial during *O. estella's* evolutionary history. Obviously the extreme harshness has selected for the unusual cave-roosting habit, the protected nest sites, a low TMES, and the ability to maintain torpor even at subfreezing temperatures. Climatic seasonality has selected for seasonality of breeding. But more exciting perhaps has been the elucidation of the difference to *O. estella* between selection pressures stemming from constant harshness as opposed to unpredictable, sudden harshness. The large body size of the species in general seems to have been determined by the sudden stormy conditions characteristic of the summer months of the year, since the storms prevent foraging for hours at a time. During the winter, though, the smaller size of the female may confer an advantage on her during the cold but stable weather when food is scarce and her total energy requirements are lower and therefore easier to meet. That her smaller size may help her survive long stable periods of food scarcity suggests that relatively greater male mortality is the reason for the skewed sex ratio during the winter and at the beginning of the breeding season. The sex ratio difference lessens as recruitment of equal numbers of males and females continues during the breeding season.

The environmental conditions of food supply and weather are identical for males and females in the winter, but the food supply is richer for the females in the summer than for the males. This is a byproduct of the precise nest-site requirements of the female and her young; the requirements are satisfied primarily in gorges with rocky outcrops. That richer food supply also occurs in the gorges is for the female a happy coincidence, but it is the nest-site requirements and limited availability that have selected for her territoriality and behavioral dominance over the male. His exclusion to the hillsides with dispersed food supplies eventually must have led to his larger size for the reasons stated above.

A factor does not have to be limiting in the sense of population regulation to act as a selection pressure. For example, predation intensity is probably relatively mild in the puna, yet the dorsal coloration of *Oreotrochilus* is probably the result of the weak selection that does exist. But the strongest selection pressures acting on individuals and populations should be those that are related to the limiting factors on population density. For *O. estella* two different factors are implicated, and they act in different seasons: nest-site limitation in the summer and energy-limitation in the winter. The number of nest sites available may determine the size of the breeding population by limiting the number of breeding females. The number of breeding males could be limited in turn by female density and the minimum area one male can occupy and still obtain both females and adequate food. At any rate, the number of females breeding is probably the single most important determinant of the number of offspring produced during the year, and thus, nest-site limitation likely determines the *potential* size of the population by the end of the breeding season. However, it must be stressed that food and climate limit winter survival and therefore determine the initial size of the breeding population at the beginning of the summer. Nest-site limitation in conjunction with energy stress in the winter determine the *actual* population size reached by the end of the breeding season. Which one of these limiting factors is more important in determining attained population size undoubtedly varies from year to year depending on the severity of the winter. Thus, it is almost impossible, and probably pointless anyway, to state a single most important limiting factor. However, since the nest-site requirements are linked directly with the climatic regime and energy demands on the female, it is reasonable to assert that the single most important category of selection pressures on *O. estella* has been energy.

Flexibility of O. estella

This species has adopted a generalist strategy for dealing with the above selection pressures. It has maintained an average wing disc loading which, in conjunction with large feet, permits flexibility of foraging technique. The flexibility of foraging technique enables it to exploit a wide range of flower types, from cactus to thistlelike flowers to more typical hummingbird flowers with tubular corollas.

It can occupy tall brush or woodland when *Colibri* is absent, or it can dwell in open puna given that a suitable roost site is nearby. Its territorial behavior is flexible and its degree of aggression varies depending on a myriad of factors. It thrives in the presence of humans and adapts its foraging and reproductive behavior to their gardens and buildings. The species gives one the impression of being vigorous and well adapted. This could have consequences for closely related species with which it co-occurs in other parts of its distribution. These consequences will be discussed in the next section.

II. THE TAXON CYCLE IN *OREOTROCHILUS*

In recent years new approaches to the study of island communities (MacArthur and Wilson, 1967; Diamond, 1973; Ricklefs and Cox, 1972) have delineated major problems in the study of the structure and function of natural communities. Two of these major problems are: what are the characteristics of a good colonizer; what effect does such an immigrant have upon the community it invades?

Many different kinds of organisms exhibit a "taxon cycle" (Wilson, 1961; Greenslade, 1968; 1969; Ricklefs, 1970; Ricklefs and Cox, 1972): a new immigrant to an island archipelago spreads vigorously among the islands (stage I), and then differentiates (stage II); extinctions follow so that the species' or group's range becomes fragmented (stage III), until in the extreme case a representative remains on only one island, and is now an endemic species (stage IV) (numbering of stages is from Ricklefs and Cox, 1972). Concurrent with these changes is a tendency to become more specialized. The most recent theory (Ricklefs and Cox, 1972) attempts to explain the apparent loss of vigor in the group by counteradaptation on the part of its prey or potential exploiters. Thus, with time, the component members of the community evolve ways to reduce the negative (exploitative) impact of the immigrant or to increase their own exploitation of it as a prey or host. This in turn lowers the immigrant's population sizes, causing susceptibility to extinction and fragmentation of distribution. Finally, the species or group in question may actually be forced to extinction by competition from still another immigrant (Ricklefs and Cox, 1972).

The high-altitude plateaus and canyons of the Peruvian and Bolivian Andes are effectively an archipelago because they are isolated from one another by ridges and valleys. Indeed, one of the early tests of the MacArthur-Wilson island equilibrium model (1967) was done on birds inhabiting páramo islands in the Andes (Vuilleumier, 1970; also see critique, Mauriello and Roskoski, 1974); this study supported the model's predictions regarding size and isolation of "islands" and showed that in fact birds treat these areas as islands. Pianka (1974) stated that "the concept underlying [the taxon cycle] presumably could be operative in mainland faunas as well as on islands. Little attempt has yet been made to interpret the ecology of mainland populations in terms of counter-adaptations." In fact, the basic idea behind the taxon cycle has previously been extended to mainlands (e.g., Dillon, 1966), but the need to extend the tests of the theory to mainland communities remains. The genus *Oreotrochilus* offers an excellent opportunity to do so.

At least occasional energy limitation among individuals is a prerequisite for any study of the mechanisms of competition for energy resources, yet this prerequisite is probably rarely satsified, or at least, rarely known to be satisfied during the term of the study. The Andean hummingbird communities satisfy this prerequisite because the environment is harsh and energy is limiting to them in the winter. This work and Carpenter (1974) have shown that: (1) flowers are scarce and poor in nectar during the winter, (2) severe hummingbird mortality probably occurs during the winter, (3) the duration and number of occurrences of energy-saving torpor increase dramatically in the hummingbirds during the winter, (4) the hummingbirds behaviorally reduce their energy output in the winter to one-third that in the summer, (5) gardens and other areas with exotic, nectar-rich flowers support many more hummingbirds during the winter than does the natural habitat, and (6) in such nectar-rich areas the hummingbirds change their behavior dramatically and their energy output approaches that of summer hummingbirds.

The distributions of the forms of *Oreotrochilus* are a classical example of a taxon cycle. The white-bellied group, characterized by *Oreotrochilus estella,* has various subspecies distributed fairly continuously along the length of the Andes from Ecuador through Peru and Bolivia to Argentina and Chile (Fig. 1). The break in its range in central Peru is likely to be an artifact of insufficient collecting; the break in northern Peru and southern Ecuador is caused by an arid, low-elevation gap in the Andes with no suitable habitat for high-montane species. If one accepts the classification of Zimmer (1951), then the subspecies of *O. estella* are from north to south: *chimborazo, stolzmanni, estella,* and *leucopleurus.* Thus, *O. estella* is probably in stage II of the taxon cycle. There are two late-stage species in the same genus, *O. melanogaster* in Peru and *O. adela* in Bolivia. These two species are much more similar to each other than to any of the subspecies of *O. estella* and probably represent fragmentations of the range of a previously widespread species that colonized the Andes before *O. estella* (see Introduction). Their ranges are so restricted relative to that of *O. estella* that they are probably approaching stage IV, the stage of endemism of one species to one isolated area. The range of *O. estella* is known to overlap that of *O. melanogaster* and the two species have been observed occupying the same habitats (Short and Moroney, 1969). Less is known about *O. adela,* but its range overlaps that of *O. estella estella* in province Potosí and Cochabamba (de Schauensee, 1966). Thus, these two overlap areas, Bolivia and Peru, are suited for a study of the processes involved in the taxon cycle.

Based on the counteradaptation principle, a hypothesis can be stated that forms of *O. estella* in provinces Potosí and Cochabamba (de Schauensee, 1966). Thus, these two overshrink. For example, parasite loads may be lighter in *O. estella* because of less time to evolve exploitation of the new species as a host, and this could give a competitive edge to *O. estella* if the two *Oreotrochilus* species are in competition. Also, the two older species may be more restricted in the range of flowers that they can exploit: the longer association with the plant community may have resulted in specialized, coevolved plant-pollinator bonds between the older species and one or a few species of plants during the breeding season. These bonds could limit the flexibility of the hummingbirds to exploit new food sources which suddenly become available, such as introduced plants in gardens, and to use other sources if the plant species upon which they depend becomes rare or extinct. A competitive advantage would be conferred onto a more flexible species in the face of environmental change. That *O. estella* may be more of a food generalist than the two older species is supported by the fact that it has a bill length (20 mm) intermediate between the very short bill of *O. melanogaster* (15 mm) and the very long bill of *O. adela* (28 mm: measurements from de Schauensee, 1970). The present investigation of the behavior and ecology of *O. estella* has clarified the fine details of the environmental selection pressures operating in their habitat in southern Peru. A similar study of the birds and environmental selection pressures in the Bolivian and central Peruvian overlap areas is needed to determine whether *O. melanogaster* and *O. adela* are "peacefully" coexisting with *O. estella* or are being outcompeted because of the processes hypothesized to be involved in the taxon cycle.

III. EVOLUTION AND COLONIZATION AT HIGH ALTITUDES

Physically harsh terrestrial environments, such as alpine and arctic regions, characteristically possess low numbers of species of animals within each major phylogenetic group, such as a class or family. For example, in the White Mountains of California and Nevada which rise to 4341 m, 115 species belonging to 33 families of birds have been regularly recorded (Hock, 1963). That is an average of 3.5 species per family. Yet only 19 species of 16 families have ranges extending above treeline (roughly at 3400 m, excluding islands of bristlecone pine). This shows extreme evenness of distribution of the high-altitude species at the family level, usually with only one species occurring per family. Furthermore, whole orders, as well as many families, are not represented at high altitude, showing unevenness of representation of higher taxa. If we look at those 19 high-altitude species, only 3 are more-or-less restricted to treeless high-altitude habitat and each represents a different family. A similar situation occurs among most vertebrate taxa in the Central American highlands (D. Futuyma, pers. comm.).

What causes this even species distribution within major taxa and uneven taxonomic representation? If one member of a family can evolve to live and reproduce at high altitude, why don't more? If we assume that most vertebrate families originated in lowland tropical or temperate regions and that wooded habitats were historically much more widespread during vertebrate evolution than forests are now, then virgin environments like tundra and high altitude were gradually invaded by members or descendents of lowland forms. The lowland tropical forms can thus be considered a "species pool" of potential colonizers. This is certainly true of the Andes, which, uplifted during the past two to ten million years, have had a relatively short time available for colonization (see also Vuilleumier, 1969b). Let us also assume that a species must undergo a long series of genetic changes to alter its way of life from existing in an environment that is physically mild but fraught with the biological dangers of predation and perhaps competition, to living in an environment where the biological dangers are reduced but the physical dangers are potentially immense. It then follows that the probability of a tropical lowland species making such a long series of genetic changes which would permit colonization of very high altitudes is quite low because the probability of the total change is the combined multiple probabilities of making each of the constituent changes. Preadaptation could increase this probability.

Occasionally, a species of some major taxon will succeed in making the change and the colonization. Once it has, given enough time, what prevents it from undergoing adaptive radiation, thereby increasing the total number of species within its family, as for example finches have done on the Galapagos (Darwin, 1859)? Tundra and high-altitude environments are simply structured, in the MacArthurs' (1961) sense. This tends to limit the opportunity for speciation, which requires heterogeneity of habitat. An increase in the number of species within the family, then, depends on yet another species in the family making long series of genetic changes. Furthermore, the total change so made must not bring the new species into direct competition with the original, or one of the two will probably become extinct, as the simple environment offers little potential for niche differentiation. Thus, the principle of competitive exclusion helps explain the evenness of distribution of species throughout families at high altitudes: (1) the change to life at high altitude is difficult to make in the first place, (2) habitat homogeneity discourages adaptive radiation in one geographic area, and (3) competitive exclusion would operate between potential new colonizers and any closely related species already established.

From this reasoning, and because the Andes are young, one can make the following predictions that are supported by information on Andean hummingbirds:

1. There will be few species of trochilids, if any, at high altitude in the Andes even though the center of the distribution of this large family occurs nearby in the lowlands to the east.

2. If there is more than one hummingbird species present, then either: (a) they will be very different with little ecological overlap, for example, generically unrelated, or else, (b) if generically related, they will be species coming from the same original colonizing stock that is invading new areas and speciating along a geographical axis. The resultant forms would tend to show clinal variations if there are gradual environmental changes along the axis of invasion. Closely related forms should be allopatric.

3. The size of the total evolutionary change required for colonization can be measured by the degree of distinction between the species that presently exist in the high-altitude area from those that exist in the low-altitude "species pool."

I will discuss the support that information available on Andean hummingbirds lends to these predictions.

1. Number of Trochilid Species

Oreotrochilus estella is the only species of hummingbird that lives year round in my study areas at 3850 m or more, compared to more than 100 species existing at those latitudes at lower altitudes (Greenewalt, 1960a: xv; Chapman, 1926), the latter making up the "species pool" available for invasion. In addition, *Colibri coruscans* is an altitude migrant that leaves for lower elevations in the winter, and *Patagona gigas* is a very rare visitor, also apparently migratory. Thus, the trend for major taxonomic groups in high-altitude areas to exhibit low numbers of species is demonstrated well by this particular family.

2. Competition and Speciation

Patagona gigas and *Oreotrochilus estella* are very different, unrelated, and essentially noncompeting in my areas. *Colibri coruscans* is also unrelated and ecologically nonoverlapping during the breeding season, the only period of time overlap with *O. estella.*

Chapman (1926) and Vuilleumier (1966) believed that most avian colonization occurred from south to north along the Andes. F. Vuilleumier (1966) believed that speciation has been encouraged by geographical periods of glaciation, and this idea was supported by the botanical work of B. Vuilleumier (1971). From central Chile to Ecuador, *Oreotrochilus* has differentiated. That the differentiation is recent is attested to by the confused state of the taxonomy of the genus and by the existence of what seem to be hybrids (Zimmer, 1951). The maximum number of species recognized is seven if all subspecies of *O. estella* are treated as species, as do Berlioz and Jouanin (1942) and Peters (1945). Of the maximum of seven species, five are roughly clinal in chromatic and size variations, and of these five, all are allopatric except *O. leucopleurus* and *O. estella* (Fig. 1). Coincidentally, there is a gradual change in climate along the Andes, the duration of the dry season decreasing with nearness to the equator. The remaining two of the seven "species" (*O. melanogaster* and *O. adela*) may have differentiated in isolation during glaciation, and may be experiencing decline from competition with forms of *O. estella*, as hypothesized in the previous section. The trend is towards confirmation of the second prediction: that if more than one hummingbird species are present, they will be either unrelated and nonoverlapping ecologically (*Patagona gigas, Colibri coruscans*), or recently evolving with clinal variations (*Oreotrochilus* species or subspecies).

3. Magnitude of the Total Evolutionary Change to Life at High Altitude

The two hummingbird species that occur year round above treeline (3650 m in southern Peru) are "atypical," as will be explained below. *Patagona gigas,* the Giant hummingbird, is the largest hummingbird, being almost twice as large as its nearest size rival (Fig. 3). Its size alone is so aberrant that this species must be considered an atypical hummingbird. Its size is adaptive to high altitude. The other species, *Oreotrochilus estella,* possesses so many morphological, physiological, and behavioral aberrancies that it, too, must be considered an atypical hummingbird. The major differences in this species are: large body size, strong feet, dull dorsal coloration, color and pattern of the male gorgette, habit of perch feeding at flowers, ability to ground feed, lack of aversion to dark places such as interiors of buildings and caves, roosting and nesting in caves and rocks, regulation of breeding population partly by nest site availability, lack of male display territory during the breeding season, highly developed female territoriality, large nest size (Dorst, 1962), nest attached to rock (Dorst, 1962), long nestling and fledgling periods, and low temperature of metabolic regulation in torpor. All of these "aberrancies" have been shown to be adaptive to the environment (present study; Dorst, 1962).

In sum, the hypothesis that there had to be a large evolutionary change in order for hummingbirds to invade this high-altitude environment is supported by the great distinctiveness of the species that have made the change.

IV. CONCLUSION

This work has examined the adaptive biology of a high-altitude hummingbird in depth. The expression of morphological, behavioral, and physiological adaptations in terms of energetics has allowed the quantification of the relative adaptive values of several of the traits of this species. I have proposed testable, quantifiable models based on energetics and suggested investigation of the interactions between the vigorously expanding and differentiating *O. estella* and the more restricted, possibly more specialized, congeneric species that overlap geographically with it. This study has shown that, although the hummingbird family does seem to be homogeneous in habits, component members of the group are capable of expanding into new and different environments and evolving quite differently from the mainstream of the family.

Literature Cited

ARMITAGE, K. B.
  1955. Territorial behavior in fall migrant Rufous Hummingbirds. Condor 57: 239-240.
BAKER, H. G., and I. BAKER
  1973. Amino-acids in nectar and their evolutionary significance. Nature 241:545.
BARTHOLOMEW, G. A., T. R. HOWELL, and T. J. CADE
  1957. Torpidity in the White-throated Swift, Anna Hummingbird, and Poor-will. Condor 59:145-155.
BENT, A. C.
  1940. Life histories of North American cuckoos, goatsuckers, hummingbirds, and their allies. U.S. Nat. Mus., Bull. 176. 506 pp.
BERGER, M.
  1974. Oxygen consumption and power of hovering hummingbirds at varying barometric and oxygen pressures. Naturwissenschaften 61:407.
BERLIOZ, J., and C. JOUANIN
  1942. Revision critique des trochilidés du genre *Oreotrochilus*. Oiseau R. F. O. 12:1-13.
BOWMAN, I.
  1916. The Andes of southern Peru. Holt and Co. 336 pp.
BROWN, J. H.
  1971. Mechanisms of competitive exclusion between two species of chipmunks. Ecology 52:305-311.
  1971. Mammals on mountaintops: nonequilibrium insular biogeography. Amer. Natur. 105:467-478.
BROWN, J. L.
  1964. The evolution of diversity in avian territorial systems. Wilson Bull. 76:160-169.
CALDER, W. A.
  1971. Temperature relationships and nesting of the Calliope Hummingbird. Condor 73:314-321.
  1973. An estimate of the heat balance of a nesting hummingbird in a chilling climate. Comp. Biochem. Physiol. 46A:291-300.
CALDER, W. A., and J. BOOSER
  1973. Hypothermia of Broad-tailed hummingbirds during incubation in nature with ecological correlations. Science 180:751-753.
CARPENTER, F. L.
  1972. Evolution and high altitude adaptation in the Andean Hillstar hummingbird. Thesis, Univ. of Calif., Berkeley.
  1974. Torpor in an Andean hummingbird: Its ecological significance. Science 183: 545-547.
CARPENTER, F. L., and R. E. MAC MILLEN
  1973. Interactions between Hawaiian honeycreepers and *Metrosideros collina* on the Island of Hawaii. I.B.P. Island Ecosystems IRP tech. report 33:1-23.
  1975. Threshold model of feeding territoriality: A test with an Hawaiian honeycreeper. I.B.P. Island Ecosystems IRP tech. rep. 61:1-11.
CHAPMAN, F. M.
  1926. The distribution of bird-life in Ecuador, a contribution to a study of the origin of Andean bird-life. Bull. Amer. Mus. Nat. Hist., v. 55. 784 pp.
CHURCHILL, D. M., and P. CHRISTENSEN
  1970. Observations on pollen harvesting by brush-tongued lorikeets. Aust. J. Zool. 18:427-437.

CODY, M. L.
  1966. A general theory of clutch size. Evolution 20:174-184.
  1968. Interspecific territoriality among hummingbird species. Condor 70:270-271.
COGSWELL, H. L.
  1949. Alternate care of two nests in the Black-chinned Hummingbird. Condor 51: 176-178.
COLWELL, R. K.
  1973. Competition and coexistence in a simple tropical community. Amer. Natur. 107:737-760.
CRUDEN, R. W.
  1972. Pollinators in high-elevation ecosystems: relative effectiveness of birds and bees. Science 176:1439-1440.
DARWIN, C.
  1859. On the Origin of Species by means of Natural Selection. Murray, London.
DE SCHAUENSEE, R. M.
  1966. The species of birds of South America and their distribution. Acad. Natur. Sci., Philadelphia, Livingston Publ. Co., Narberth, Penn. 577 pp.
  1970. A guide to the birds of South America. Acad. Natur. Sci., Philadelphia, Livingston Publ. Co., Narberth, Penn. 470 pp.
DIAMOND, J. M.
  1973. Distribution ecology of New Guinea birds. Science 179:759-769.
DILLON, L. S.
  1966. The life cycle of the species: an extension of current concepts. Syst. Zool. 15:112-126.
DORST, J.
  1956. Etude biologique des trochilidés des hauts plateaux péruvians. Oiseau R. F. O. 26:165-193.
  1962. Nouvelles recherches biologiques sur les trochilidés des hautes Andes péruviennes (*Oreotrochilus estella*). Oiseau R. F. O. 32:95-126.
EPTING, R. J., and T. M. CASEY
  1973. Power output and wing disc loading in hovering hummingbirds. Amer. Natur. 107:761-765.
EWALD, P., and F. L. CARPENTER
  Energy controls over feeding territoriality in the Anna hummingbird. In prep.
FRENCH, N. R., and R. W. HODGES
  1959. Torpidity in cave-roosting hummingbirds. Condor 61:223.
GADGIL, M., and W. H. BOSSERT
  1970. Life historical consequences of natural selection. Amer. Natur. 104:1-24.
GATES, D. M.
  1962. Energy Exchange in the Biosphere. Harper and Row, Inc., New York.
GILBERT, L. E.
  1972. Pollen feeding and reproductive biology of *Heliconius* butterflies. Proc. Nat. Acad. Sci. 69:1403-1407.
GOULD, J.
  1861. Monograph of the Trochilidae. 5 vols. London.
GRANT, K. A., and V. GRANT
  1968. Hummingbirds and their flowers. Columbia Univ. Press, New York. 115 pp.
GREENEWALT, C. H.
  1960a. Hummingbirds. Doubleday and Co., Garden City, N.Y. 250 pp.
  1960b. Dimensional relationships for flying animals. Private publ.

GREENSLADE, P. J. M.
1968. Island patterns in the Solomon Islands bird fauna. Evolution 22:751-761.
1969. Land fauna; insect distribution patterns in the Solomon Islands. Phil. Trans. R. Soc. B 255:271-284.

HAINSWORTH, F. R., and L. L. WOLF
1970. Regulation of oxygen consumption and body temperature during torpor in a hummingbird, *Eulampis jugularis.* Science 168:368-369.
1972. Power for hovering flight in relation to body size in hummingbirds. Amer. Natur. 106:589-596.

HEINRICH, B., and P. H. RAVEN
1972. Energetics and pollination ecology. Science 176:597-602.

HERREID, C. F. II, and B. KESSEL
1967. Thermal conductance in birds and mammals. Comp. Biochem. Physiol. 21:405-414.

HOCK, R. J.
1963. Birds of the White Mountain Range, California. Univ. of Calif., White Mountain Research Station. 9 pp.

HOLLINGWORTH, S. E., and R. W. R. RUTLAND
1968. Studies of Andean uplift. Part I. Post-Cretaceous evolution of the San Bartolo area, North Chile. Geol. J. 6:49-62.

HOWELL, T. R., and W. R. DAWSON
1954. Nest temperatures and attentiveness in the Anna hummingbird. Condor 56:93-97.

JOHNSON, A. W.
1965. The birds of Chile and adjacent regions of Argentina, Bolivia and Peru. Vol. I. Platt Establecimientos Gráficos S. A., Buenos Aires. 398 pp.
1967. The birds of Chile and adjacent regions of Argentina, Bolivia and Peru. Vol. II. Platt Establecimientos Gráficos S. A., Buenos Aires. 447 pp.

JONES, R. E., and A. S. LEOPOLD
1967. Nesting interference in a dense population of Wood Ducks. J. Wildl. Mgmt. 31:221-228.

KEAST, A.
1968. Seasonal movements in the Australian Honeyeaters (Meliphagidae) and their ecological significance. Emu 67:159-209.

KNOCH, K.
1930. Klimakunde von Südamerika. *In:* Handbuch der Klimatologie, t. II, parte G, ed. W. Köppen, and R. Geiger, Berlin.

KOEPCKE, M.
1964. Las aves del departamento de Lima. Lima, Peru. 118 pp.

KREBS, C. J.
1972. Ecology; the experimental analysis of distribution and abundance. Harper and Row, Inc., New York. 694 pp.

LACK, D.
1968. *Ecological adaptations for breeding in birds.* Methuen and Co., London. 409 pp.

LANGNER, S.
1973. Zur Biologie des Hockland Kolibris *Oreotrochilus estella* in den Anden Boliviens. Bonn. Zool. Beitr. 1/2:24-47.

LASIEWSKI. R. C.
1962. The capture and maintenance of hummingbirds for experimental purposes. Avicult. Mag. 68:59-64.

1963. Oxygen consumption of torpid, resting, active, and flying hummingbirds. Physiol. Zool. 36:122-140.

1964. Body temperatures, heart and breathing rate, and evaporative water loss in hummingbirds. Physiol. Zool. 37:212-223.

LASIEWSKI, R. C., and R. J. LASIEWSKI
1967. Physiological responses of the Blue-throated and Rivoli's Hummingbirds. Auk 84:34-48.

LASIEWSKI, R. C., W. W. WEATHERS, and M. H. BERNSTEIN
1967. Physiological responses of the Giant Hummingbird, *Patagona gigas*. Comp. Biochem. Physiol. 23:797-813.

LEGG, K., and F. A. PITELKA
1956. Ecologic overlap of Allen and Anna Hummingbirds nesting at Santa Cruz, California. Condor 58:393-405.

LEVIN, D. A., and W. W. ANDERSON
1970. Competition for pollinators between simultaneously flowering species. Amer. Natur. 104:455-468.

MC NAB, B. K.
1971. On the ecological significance of Bergmann's Rule. Ecology 52:845-854.

MAC ARTHUR, R. H.
1972. Geographical ecology. Harper and Row, Inc., New York. 269 pp.

MAC ARTHUR, R. H., and J. W. MAC ARTHUR
1961. On bird species diversity. Ecology 42:594-598.

MAC ARTHUR, R. H., and E. O. WILSON
1967. The theory of island biogeography. Princeton Univ. Press, New Jersey. 203 pp.

MAC MILLEN, R. E., and F. L. CARPENTER
Plant-animal interactions on the island of Hawaii. In prep.

MARSHALL, A. J. (ed.)
1961. Biology and comparative physiology of birds. Vol. II. Academic Press, New York. 468 pp.

MAURIELLO, D., and J. P. ROSKOSKI
1974. A reanalysis of Vuilleumier's data. Amer. Natur. 108:711-714.

MORSE, D. H.
1974. Niche breadth as a function of social dominance. Amer. Natur. 108:818-830.

NICHOLSON, E. M.
1931. Field notes on the Guiana King Hummingbird. Ibis, ser. 13, 1:534-553.

PEARSON, O. P.
1950. The metabolism of hummingbirds. Condor 52:145-152.
1953. Use of caves by hummingbirds and other species at high altitudes in Peru. Condor 55:17-20.
1954. The daily energy requirements of a wild Anna Hummingbird. Condor 56:317-322.

PEÑA, L. E., J. ROTTMANN, and G. BARRIA.
1964. Observaciones ornitologicas. Rev. Chilena Hist. Nat. 55:109-114.

PENNYCUICK, C. J.
1968. Power requirements for horizontal flight in the pigeon, *Columba livia*. J. Exp. Biol. 49:527-555.
1969. The mechanics of bird migration. Ibis 111:525-556.

PERCIVAL, M. S.
1965. Floral biology. Pergamon Press, Oxford. 243 pp.

PETERS, J. L.
　1945. Check-list of birds of the world. Vol. V. Harvard Univ. Press, Cambridge. 306 pp.
PIANKA, E. R.
　1974. Evolutionary ecology. Harper and Row, New York. 356 pp.
PITELKA, F. A.
　1942. Territoriality and related problems in North American hummingbirds. Condor 44: 189-204.
　1951. Ecologic overlap and interspecific strife in breeding populations of Anna and Allen Hummingbirds. Ecology 32:641-661.
POUGH, F. H.
　1973. Lizard energetics and diet. Ecology 54:837-844.
RECHER, H. F.
　1969. Bird species diversity and habitat diversity in Australia and North America. Amer. Natur. 103:75-80.
RHOADS, S. N.
　1912. Birds of the páramo of central Ecuador. Auk 29:141-149.
RICKLEFS, R. E.
　1970. Clutch size in birds: outcome of opposing predator and prey adaptations. Science 168:599-600.
　1970. Stage of taxon cycle and distribution of birds on Jamaica, Greater Antilles. Evolution 24:475-477.
RICKLEFS, R. E., and G. W. COX
　1972. Taxon cycles in the West Indian avifauna. Amer. Natur. 106:195-219.
RUSCHI, A.
　1949. A polinizacão realizada pelos Trochilideos, a sua área de alimentacão e o repovoamento. Bol. Mus. Biol. Prof. Mello – Leitão 2:1-51.
　1961a. Algumas observacões sôbre: *Oreotrochilus estella chimborazo* (De Lattre and Bourcier) e *Oreotrochilus estella jamensonii* Jardine, Bol. Mus. Biol., Santa Teresa, Esp. Santo, Brasil, no. 24:1-10.
　1961b. Algumas observacões sôbre *Oxypogon guerinii lindenii* (Parzudaki) (Aves). Bol. Mus. Biol., Santa Teresa, Esp. Santo, Brasil, no. 29:1-9.
　1967. Beija-flores das matas, dos scrubs, das savanas, dos campos e grasslands do Brasil, e a sua zoogeografia. Bol. Mus. Biol., Santa Teresa, Esp. Santo, Brasil, no. 51:1-23.
SCHMIDT-NIELSEN, K.
　1972. Locomotion: Energy cost of swimming, flying, and running. Science 177: 222-228.
SCHOENER, T. W.
　1971. Large-billed insectivorous birds: a precipitous diversity gradient. Condor 73: 154-161.
SHORT, L. L., and J. J. MORONEY
　1969. Notes on some birds of central Peru. Bull. British Ornith. Club 89:112-115.
SKEAD, D. M.
　1963. Gurney's Sugarbird, *Promerops gurneyi* Verreaux. *In:* The Natal Drakensberg, Ostrich 34:160-164.
　1967. The Sunbirds of southern Africa. South African Bird Book Fund, Cape and Transvaal Printers, Ltd., Capetown. 351 pp.
SKUTCH, A. F.
　1940. Accounts *in* Life histories of North American cuckoos, goatsuckers, hummingbirds, and their allies, A. C. Bent, U. S. Nat. Mus., Bull. 176, 506 pp.

1951. Life history of Longuemare's Hermit Hummingbird. Ibis 93:180-195.
1964. Life history of the Scaly-breasted Hummingbird. Condor 66:186-198.
1973. The life of hummingbirds. Crown Publ., Inc., New York. 95 pp.

SMITH, G. T. C.
1969. A high altitude hummingbird on the volcano Cotopaxi. Ibis 111:17-22.

SNOW, B. K.
1974. Lek behaviour and breeding of Guy's Hermit Hummingbird *Phaethornis guy*. Ibis 116:278-297.

SNOW, B. K., and D. W. SNOW
1971. The feeding ecology of tanagers and honeycreepers in Trinidad. Auk 88:291-322.

SNOW, D. W.
1968. The singing assemblies of Little Hermits. Living Bird 7:47-55.

STILES, F. G.
1971. Time, energy, and territoriality of the Anna Hummingbird (*Calypte anna*). Science 173:818-821.
1973. Food supply and the annual cycle of the Anna Hummingbird. Univ. of Calif. Publications in Zoology 97:1-109.

STILES, F. G., and L. L. WOLF
1970. Hummingbird territoriality at a tropical flowering tree. Auk 87:467-491.

TORDOFF, H. B.
1966. Torpidity in montane hummingbirds. Organization for Tropical Studies, San José, Costa Rica. 2 pp.

TUCKER, V. A.
1968. Respiratory exchange and evaporative water loss in the flying budgerigar. J. Exp. Biol. 48:67-87.
1970. Energetic cost of locomotion in animals. Comp. Biochem. Physiol. 34:841-846.

VERBEEK, N. A. M.
1971. Hummingbirds feeding on sand. Condor 73:112-113.

VUILLEUMIER, B. S.
1971. Pleistocene changes in the fauna and flora of South America. Science 173:771-780.

VUILLEUMIER, F.
1966. Speciation in the high Andean birds. Ph.D. diss. Harvard Univ.
1969a. Field notes on some birds from the Bolivian Andes. Ibis 111:599-608.
1969b. Pleistocene speciation in birds living in the high Andes. Nature 223:1179-1180.
1970. Insular biogeography in continental regions. The northern Andes of South America. Amer. Natur. 104:373-388.

WEBERBAUER, A.
1945. El mundo vegetal de los Andes Peruanos. Ministerio de Agricultura, Lima. 776 pp.

WAGNER, H. O.
1945. Notes on the life history of the Mexican Violet-ear. Wilson Bull. 57:165-187.

WILSON, E. O.
1961. The nature of the taxon cycle in the Melanesian ant fauna. Amer. Nat. 95:169-193.

WOLF, L. L.
1967. A study of hummingbird torpidity. Organization for Tropical Studies, San José, Costa Rica. 3 pp.
1969. Female territoriality in a tropical hummingbird. Auk 86:490-504.
1970. The impact of seasonal flowering on the biology of some tropical hummingbirds. Condor 72:1-14.

WOLF, L. L., and F. R. HAINSWORTH
  1971. Time and energy budgets of territorial hummingbirds. Ecology 52:980-988.
  1972. Environmental influence on regulated body temperature in torpid hummingbirds. Comp. Biochem. Physiol. 41A:167-173.
WOLF, L. L., F. R. HAINSWORTH, and F. G. STILES
  1972. Energetics of foraging: rate and efficiency of nectar extraction by hummingbirds. Science 176:1351-1352.
WOLF, L. L., and F. G. STILES
  1970. Evolution of pair cooperation in a tropical hummingbird. Evolution 24:759-773.
ZIMMER, J. T.
  1951. Studies of Peruvian birds, no. 60. Amer. Mus. Novitates, No. 1513. 45 pp.

PLATES

Two of the plants used by *O. estella* in the summer breeding season: a. *Cajophora (rosulata?)*, showing the five large, white nectaries. Photograph is to scale. b. *Bomarea dulcis* to scale. Plants identified by Dr. R. Ferreyra.

Chuquiraga spinosa, used by *O. estella* mainly in the winter nonbreeding season. a. A branch, showing several inflorescences; 1/4 natural size. b. Single flower head, showing exerted styles; 1.5 x natural size. Identified by Dr. R. Ferreyra.

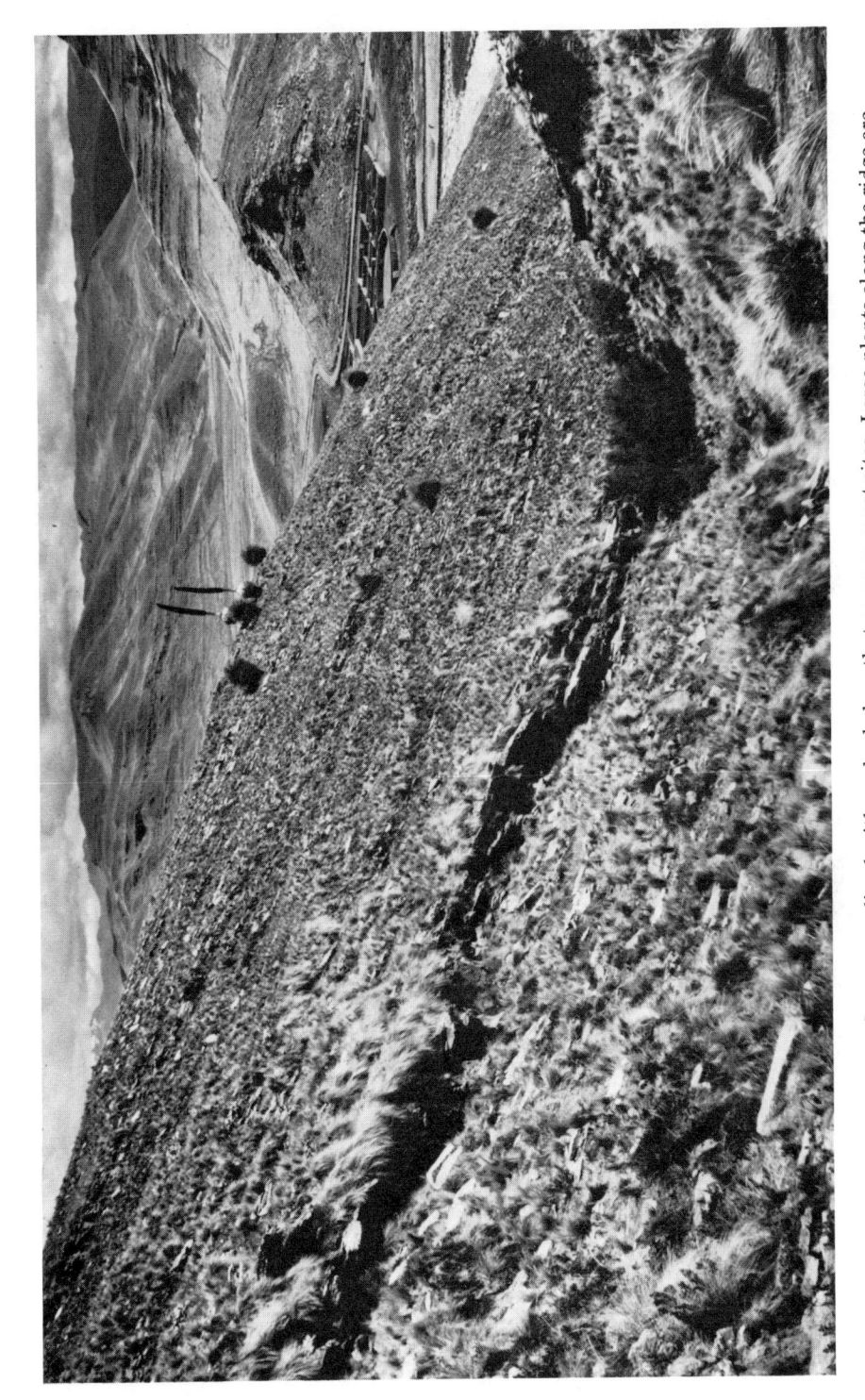

Summer roosting area. Open gorge lined with rocky ledges that serve as roost sites. Large plants along the ridge are *Puya raimondi* (Bromeliaceae), the underside of whose fronds may serve as nesting sites.

Winter roosting site. Large rock outcrop with deep vertical crevices and caves where five hummingbirds were found roosting.

Female breeding season territories. A solitary female breeding territory. Her nest is indicated by the x in the rock outcrop. She defended the brushy gorge below and to the right of her nest, all of the hillside within view of the photograph, and another 30 m of hillside and gorge to the left out of view of the photograph. Her nearest neighbor had a nest under a rock ledge just behind the shrub indicated by an arrow and x.

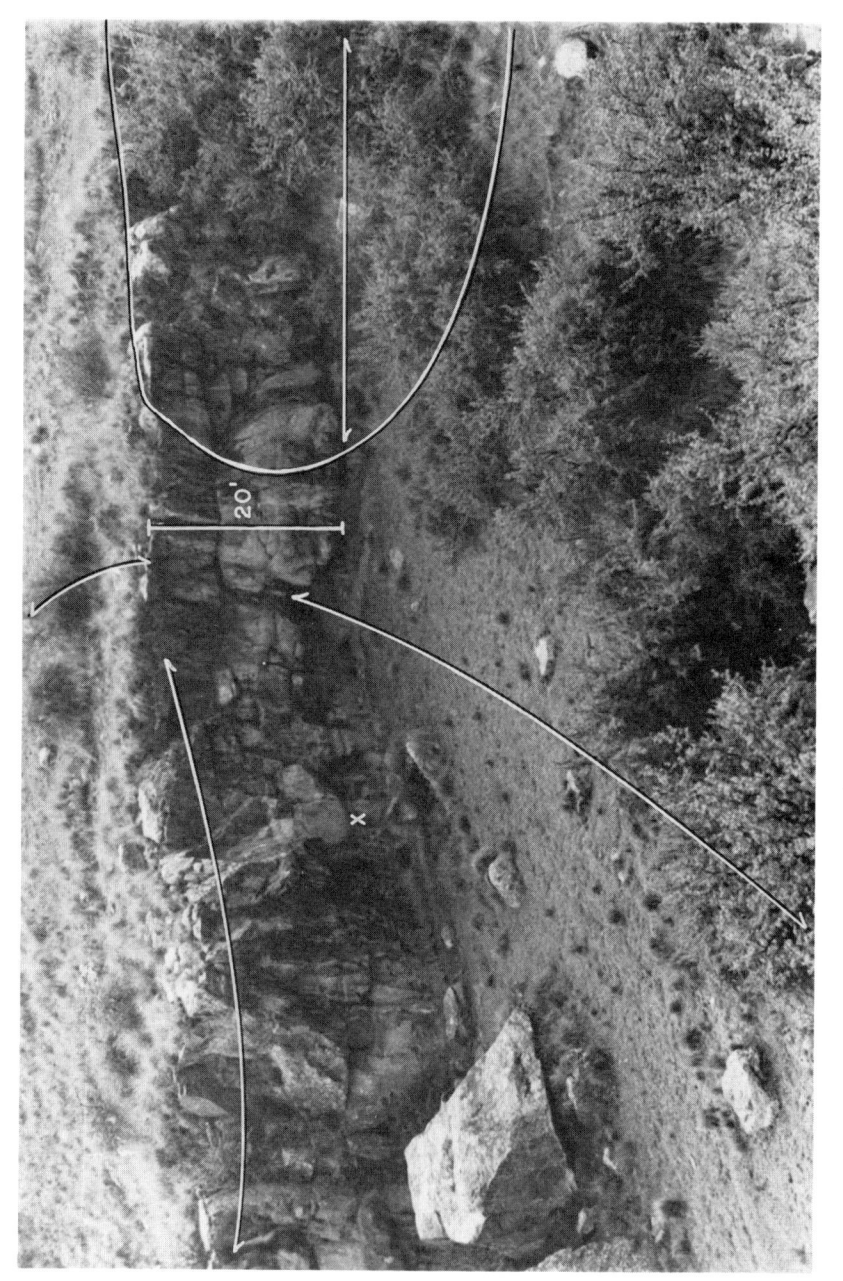

Semicolonial nesting area. Paths of access to four of five nests are indicated by lines with arrows. Arrowheads ending at the edge of the photograph point to the directions in which each of these females flew to feed separately from the nesting area. The arrowheads ending in the face of the rock outcrop indicate each of the four nest sites; the x marks a fifth occupied nest that was destroyed before I was able to make observations. The intermediate-size territory of the female with the nest furthest to the right in the photograph is indicated by outlining.

Winter feeding territories in *Eucalyptus*. The territories of each of four hummingbirds are indicated by outlining. Two areas of overlap that exhibited particularly intense territorial strife are shown. The birds defended about two trees each. The trees varied from 20 to 30 m tall. From left to right, the territories were defended by: a female, a female, a male, a female.

Male *Oreotrochilus estella* clinging in winter nocturnal torpor to a rafter beam in a barn at Hacienda Calacala, Peru.

WITHDRAWN